# *Elevate*

## YOUR
## LIFE AT HOME

Inspiring Ideas to Add Joy, Peace
and Magic to Your Homelife

JENNIFER MELVILLE

# OTHER BOOKS BY JENNIFER MELVILLE

*Elevate the Everyday:*
*Actions and Ideas to Enhance the Experience of Daily Life*

*Elevate Your Personal Style:*
*Inspiration for the Everyday Woman*

*Elevate Your Health:*
*Inspiration and Motivation to Embrace and Maintain a Healthy Lifestyle*

*Preloved Chic:*
*Stylish Secrets to Elevate Your Wardrobe With Second-Hand Fashion*

# DEDICATION

*For my family,*

*Thank you for filling our home with love.*

# CONTENTS

# INTRODUCTION

Hello! Thank you so much for picking up this little book of mine. My guess is you were drawn to the title because, like me, you enjoy seeking ways to add more peace, enjoyment and magic to your life.

Since "home is where the heart is", it's a great place to zone in our attention. The worldwide pandemic certainly drew our focus inward, and for many, life at home became more important than ever before. Why not seek out ways to make living in the various corners of our homes as pleasurable as possible? My experience has been that even the smallest of intentional actions can make a huge impact on the quality of our homelife.

I don't profess to be an expert on the art of living. I'm not one of those polished lifestyle bloggers with a picture-perfect Instagram feed. I don't have any training in home decorating or design. I'm an everyday woman, just like you I suspect. I'm a professional accountant by trade, but more importantly, I'm a mother, wife, daughter, sister and friend.

I'm also a homebody, and have been my entire life. For as long as I can remember, I have been tweaking my surroundings to make them more beautiful, peaceful, efficient, and organized. Starting in on this book, I quickly realized I've been preparing to write it ever since I was a little girl. As a child, my bedroom was my castle, my hideout and my secret garden. I spent countless hours behind those four walls; decorating, primping, rearranging and organizing!

The accountant in me enjoys approaching my life with an analytical mind; drawing on the wisdom of others and then asking, "What does this mean to me? How can I apply this concept or idea to my messy, modern life as an everyday woman?"

Although a lot of lifestyle books on the market have a dreamy quality to them, at times their ideas feel impractical or impossible to everyday women like us. I hope that with my realistic view on life, (and a heavy dose of humor) I am able to provide a point of view that feels a bit more practical and attainable to the masses.

*Elevating Your Life at Home* is not just about beautifying your surroundings. It's also about how you and your family *live in* and *interact with* the spaces of your home. Although we are all unique individuals, in many ways we are all the same. Homebody or not, we all need a place to come home to at the end of the day to unwind, reset and replenish our souls.

The purpose of this book is to inspire you to view your homelife with a fresh perspective. My hope is that it jumpstarts a sense of enthusiasm within you to add more beauty and magic to your life at home. My ideas aren't necessarily new or groundbreaking, but they do offer my own personal spin and touch on things. (I also believe there are a few original and glittering gems hidden between these pages!) They are meant to serve as food for thought to get your own creative juices flowing. I hope my words inspire you to take action on creating a life at home that feels peaceful, soothing, fulfilling and beautiful; one that allows you to connect more meaningfully with not only those you love, but with yourself as well.

As always, I recommend my books be enjoyed with a pretty journal close at hand. As you make your way through the pages, there will be many opportunities to reflect and record your *own* ideas on how to elevate *your* life at home. I'm a big believer that we need to capture moments of brilliance as soon as they pop in our heads. A journal serves as a safe place to store them, so they won't be forgotten and lost forever!

So please, tuck yourself in the coziest and most comfortable nook you can find, and let's get started on elevating your life at home!

# 1

# SPRINKLE YOUR HOME
# WITH FAIRY DUST

I was lucky enough to grow up with a fairy of sorts—my mom! She is one of those people who loves giving gifts and sprinkling the lives of those she loves with tiny surprises. It wasn't uncommon to pull down the bed covers at night and find a tiny treasure hiding under my pillow. It might have been a pack of stickers, a hair ribbon, or a handful of peppermints. They were always just simple little treats, but I was genuinely delighted each time I discovered them. In fact, I probably have fonder memories of these everyday treasure hunts than visits from Santa or the Easter Bunny (which of course was also Mom, but these holidays were rife with expectation). Her everyday surprises were special, unexpected, tiny, and yet extraordinary. I didn't realize it at the time, but these little acts of generosity and thoughtfulness were one of the many ways she sought to elevate *my* everyday.

As a grandmother, she continues to sprinkle her fairy dust on a regular basis. My boys might be considered young men now at the ages of fifteen and sixteen, but they still race through her house upon arrival to check out all her regular hiding spots. They are usually rewarded by some chocolate truffles or a few macarons from her friend Jean-Pierre, a real French pâtissier. She discreetly slips me my personal stash of peppermints, so the boys don't get their sticky fingers on them!

I like to think that a little bit of Mom's fairy dust rubbed off on me. In fact, when I became a mother, I bestowed upon myself the title of "The Wool Fairy". At the time, I was passionate about offering my children beautiful, open-ended toys that encouraged creative and imaginative play (more on this in chapter 2). I learned how to knit and crochet so I could make these toys myself. My efforts began in the play kitchen, where I tackled filling the cupboards with a charming selection of woolen fruits and vegetables. I'd spend my evenings mastering a new variety from the garden, and my son would wake up to a little woolen treasure under his pillow. I even turned The Wool Fairy into a small business venture, selling my woolly play food on Etsy and at local shops and markets. At the time, it was rewarding to imagine that my delightful little creations were adding a touch of fairy magic to the toy boxes of other children.

Do you ever find yourself missing those whimsical days of childhood when we all believed in magic? Why wait for a secret fairy to come knocking on your door? Why not adopt a fairy mindset as you go about your everyday life? Sprinkle *your life* with hidden gems, to be forgotten and rediscovered or appreciated at a later date. Wouldn't it be fun to think of your own home as a treasure chest of surprises? It's a unique and entertaining approach to express self-love and elevate an ordinary day.

I realize this whole concept might seem a bit frivolous and flowery, but the idea is to just have fun with it. I'm not as crazy as I sound in this chapter! (Keep in mind, I am a practical accountant.) There is definitely room in all our lives for a bit more fantasy and whimsy!

Grab a journal and brainstorm a list of fun and creative ideas. Think of things that would truly bring you pleasure when you encounter them unexpectedly in a secret hiding spot.

## Stash Some Cash

Who hasn't delighted in the unanticipated discovery of long-forgotten cash? Let's be honest, money is always at the top of everyone's wish list! The next time you store your winter coat or seasonal handbag, why not slip a twenty-dollar bill (or more if you can spare it) into the inside pocket? Imagine the small thrill next season when you reach inside and grasp that crispy bill. Treat yourself to something indulgent with it—an overpriced specialty coffee, or a new shade of lipstick to brighten up your makeup bag. (On another note, be sure to check the pockets of coats before placing them in storage. I once found a lost key fob to our vehicle hiding in a winter jacket, which I paid over $500 to replace a few months prior!)

## Make Use of Memorabilia

Do you have a collection of favorite books that you pick up and flip through on a regular basis? I'm definitely a big fan of eBooks, but I also have a special selection of inspiring hard copy titles that I refer to frequently. I reread *Gift from the Sea* by Anne Morrow Lindberg every single summer during our beach vacation at the family cottage. I know it inside out, but somehow, I still manage to glean new wisdom from her words every time I pick it up. I enjoy this book even more when I'm pleasantly surprised by something special tucked between the pages.

Slipping mementos into the pages of your much-loved books is another fun way to inject a lovely surprise into an ordinary moment. Love notes, thoughtful greeting cards, pretty postcards and children's artwork all make great bookmarks! I recently discovered a little thank-you note hiding in a book that my son wrote to me when he was nine years old. My heart melted at the sight of it. I was flooded with fond memories of a little boy who was once obsessed with tropical birds, and had painstakingly documented all his favorite species for me with neatly labelled drawings. This heartwarming reminder of my love for him definitely elevated my mood in the moment.

Pressing delicate flowers is another way to add a sweet surprise inside the pages of your library. Spring violets are one of my favorites to preserve. Any time I stumble across a four-leaf clover in my travels, I always make sure to press it between the pages of a book from my library. I'll never pass up the opportunity to grant myself a bit of extra luck in the future!

## Rotate Your Belongings

Treats and surprises don't have to be something new and novel. They can often be a much-loved object that you haven't seen in a while. The expression, "absence makes the heart grow fonder" doesn't just apply to one's love life.

I first experimented with this concept when I had young children. I found that only displaying a small selection of their toys left them with fewer choices. As a result, they were less distracted and overwhelmed, and more likely to become absorbed in the activity they had chosen. It also helped keep the clutter down in my living room! Pulling a toy out of storage sparked renewed enthusiasm and interest in it. In a sense, it became *new* to them all over again! This approach kept the toy box fresh, uncluttered and engaging.

You can extend this concept well beyond the toy box and incorporate it into many areas of your home. It's easy to wrap your head around this idea with seasonal items in your life. I use this approach the most in my closet, as I only have the current season's clothes on display. Everything else is tucked away in a storage bin in the hall closet. When the seasons change and it's time to switch things up, I genuinely feel a tingle of excitement as I pull some of my favorite pieces from the bin. Just like the toys, these items feel new and exciting. My fresh wardrobe is a harbinger of the deliciousness of the upcoming season!

Home décor items also lend well to this concept. We all have a collection of favorite decorative objects and mementoes, but there is no rule that they all have to be on display at one time. Anything you own, from vases, coffee table books to throw pillows, can be tucked away in storage for a period of time. Do a scan of your rooms and identify areas that feel a tad cluttered. Clear the area completely, then only return a few of the items to the original space. Stash the rest away to be rediscovered in a month or two. You will find that you love them even more after taking a visual break and then reinviting them back into your living space.

# Store Seasonal Items Nicely

When it comes time to tuck an item away for a period of "rest", I like to do so in a caring and loving manner. That way, when I rustle it from hibernation, it appears well rested, fresh and almost brand new! It truly feels like unwrapping a gift!

I take the time and effort to wash or dry clean my clothing before storing it for the season. I polish and condition my footwear and leather handbags. I tend to any maintenance issues, such as loose buttons and threads or unravelling seams. I store things as nicely as possible by folding them neatly, returning them to their original boxes and dust bags, or hanging them in garment bags.

I take the same approach when storing decorative objects such as holiday ornaments. My Christmas tree decorations hold a very special place in my heart, as many of them are handmade and one of a kind. Instead of dumping them all hurriedly in a box, (which by the time the holidays are over, is extremely tempting to do) I carefully sort them by type into little boxes. I wrap the most fragile ones in pretty tissue paper. The following year, it's always a lovely and elevating experience to open the neatly arranged box and unwrap those tiny packages to reveal the precious ornaments inside.

# Plant Something

Do you marvel at the magic of seeds as I do? It is hard to believe that such a tiny unremarkable speck can grow into a flourishing and beautiful plant. Go ahead and plant something, and enjoy watching the magic unfold!

Last fall I came up with the brilliant idea to purchase one hundred tulip bulbs. It seemed like a great idea, until I found myself faced with the arduous task of planting them before the ground froze. I procrastinated until the final hour. Grumpy, cold and rushed, I finally dragged myself outside on a chilly November morning and pretty much tossed them haphazardly into my flower beds. I was convinced that the bad karma I was exuding while planting them was going to lead to lackluster results come spring. It turns out Mother Nature ignored my negative attitude, and rewarded me with a brilliant and uplifting array of tulips when the snow melted. The blooms were especially appreciated because they arrived when I needed a boost the most; during the exhausting third round of pandemic lockdowns in our area.

Do you have a corner of the yard that you could tuck in a few bulbs? It might feel like a bit of effort at the time, but those little gems will definitely elevate your day when they magically reveal their beauty months down the road.

# Get Creative With Your Hiding Spots

One skill any real fairy possesses is the ability to identify the perfect hiding spot! This may sound odd and unexpected, but my freezer is one of my favorite treasure chests!

Most afternoons with my cup of tea, I enjoy a single chocolate peanut butter ball made by a local woman. They are special, decadent, and definitely on the expensive side! They are meant to be savored and enjoyed one at a time. My son, who shares in my love for them, believes they are best consumed by the dozen! I had to start hiding them from him, and the darkest corner of the freezer seemed like the best spot available. When he sniffed out my secret stash, I went the extra step to store them in a plastic container labelled "pasta sauce". He has yet to figure this out. I do share them with him now and then, (I'm not that selfish) but I delight in the idea that there is a special treat hidden away, waiting just for me!

Could your freezer serve as a treasure chest as well? Not only is it a wonderful hiding spot, it serves as a great tool in keeping yourself from binging on sweet treats. Freezing them, and taking them out one at a time, takes more effort and makes them less accessible to scarf down without thinking.

Freezer treats don't always have to cater to your sweet tooth. It's all about your perspective on what constitutes a treat. Why not double up on that lasagna recipe and tuck one into the freezer? After a long, exhausting day, a homemade meal hiding in the ice box can truly feel like a gift from your fairy godmother!

## Be Generous

The spirit of a fairy is of course, one of generosity. By sprinkling your fairy dust on the lives of others, the universe will no doubt reward you! There is a lot of truth to the notion that there is more joy in giving than receiving. Be sure to include loved ones (and even strangers!) in your delivery of treats. It's a win-win scenario as you will be elevating your own day along with theirs.

Sneak a short love note into your husband's laptop when he's not looking. Imagine how he will feel when faced with a busy day at the office, he opens it up and discovers your thoughtful comments about how much he is appreciated. Do you remember a time when our mailboxes included personal letters instead of just junk mail and bills? Why not send a cute card to someone via good old-fashioned snail mail? Drop an unexpected pack of Tic Tacs in your child's lunch. Add a few percentage points on the tip of the well-deserving server. If someone in your family is going on a trip, hide something special in their suitcase!

I went on a two-week cycling holiday to Croatia with my father a couple of years ago. It was the first time I had ever left my children for more than two nights! Although exciting, it was also stressful and nerve wracking to leave everyone behind. When I pulled into my hotel room utterly exhausted, I was greeted by a sweet little hand painted rock from my family in my suitcase. This was another one of those heart-melting moments.

The possibilities are endless with this one, so have fun dreaming up and actually following through on some of these quick and easy acts of thoughtfulness. They might be tiny in effort, but the impacts can be huge.

## ELEVATING ACTIONS AND INSPIRATION

- Become your own personal fairy by tucking away a few treats and treasures for yourself, to be forgotten and rediscovered at a later date.
- Have fun coming up with a list of easy, simple and delightful treats for yourself that you would genuinely enjoy receiving. Get busy and start sprinkling!
- Slip a few crispy bills into an object that you will most certainly reach for in a few months. Seasonal purses and coats make great choices. When you "discover" this extra cash down the road, be sure to indulge in something decadent with it.

- Instead of storing mementos in a dusty shoebox at the top of your closet, hide them in spots you visit on a fairly regular basis. Enjoy the elevating boost you receive when you stumble across a special photo, love note or piece of child's artwork. Books are my favorite place to hide these types of goodies, but I've also been known to add a few to my underwear drawer!

- Rotate those belongings you choose to display in your home to keep your environment feeling fresh and new. It's even worthwhile to take a break from some of your most beloved items. When you dust them off from storage in a month or two, you will cherish and appreciate them even more.

- Anytime you place an object in storage, do so with a kind and tender touch. Be sure to tend to any maintenance issues before tucking an object away. Instead of dumping them in a box in the basement or garage, take a few moments to sort and store them nicely. Make use of tissue paper, dust covers, garment bags and original boxes to keep them clean and in top condition.

- If your outdoor living space allows for it, find a spot to plant a few fall bulbs or perennials. By getting your hands dirty and making a little upfront effort, you will be rewarded months down the road by beautiful blooms.

- Get creative with your hiding spots. The household freezer is a great place to store (hide) your secret stash of sweet treats. It's also a true gift to oneself to have a freezer stocked with healthy meals that you can pull out on a moment's notice.

- Treat others with a generous heart. Look for ways to extend your fairy mindset to the ones you love. Small acts of appreciation and kindness can make a huge impact. (I hope my own mother knows just how much I have appreciated her magical touch over the years!)

# 2

# CHOOSE BEAUTY

A few years ago, my family and I were fortunate enough to travel to the south of France on what I considered to be my dream vacation. We set ourselves up in a quaint Airbnb just outside the medieval village of Ménerbes (the setting for Peter Mayle's *A Year in Provence*). With this as our home base, we ventured out each day on little excursions to explore the surrounding area of the Luberon region.

Regardless of our plans for the day, I always made sure to get up extra early so I could venture out on my own for a morning run in the Provençal countryside. I looked forward to these solitary outings because they gave me a chance to explore my surroundings at my own pace (and without the distraction of complaining teenagers in the background). I especially loved sneaking down the odd overgrown path shooting off the side of the road. These meandering trails often lead me under a canopy of ancient trees, between the rows of vineyards, or to the doorstep of a beautifully crumbling stone building. I was frankly awestruck by my surroundings. (We don't have many medieval villages to roam here in Canada.) Honestly, I would most accurately describe the feeling as being drunk on beauty. I was *that* taken aback by it. (There was no need for a glass of rosé to get giddy.)

One morning, I noticed a sweet little roadside stone structure off in the distance. As I approached, I decided it was worth investigating! Might this be an ancient garden shed, a timeworn animal stall, or some special hut specific to the wine making industry? I was intrigued! To my shock, it turned out to be the local garbage and recycling station! It was in that moment that I was convinced that the French truly are the world experts on the art of adding beauty to everyday life.

I came home from that trip more determined than ever to tap into my inner French girl and surround myself with as much beauty as possible. If they could turn their trash station into a work of art, surely I could up my game in a few key areas of my life!

## Permit Yourself to Indulge in Beauty

I tend to believe that humans have a lot in common with honey bees and hummingbirds. Just as these tiny creatures are naturally drawn to beautiful flowers, we too instinctively gravitate towards pretty things.

Adding beauty to my surroundings has been on my agenda since childhood. From a very young age, I spent hours rearranging my bedroom furniture, creating artful displays of my knickknacks, and organizing my drawers. I was even able to snag my teen dream job in high school working at a local gift shop. I couldn't believe I was getting paid to spend my days sniffing scented candles and dreaming up attractive display shelves. (With my generous employee discount to tempt me, most of my paycheck went to acquiring even more pretty things!)

Somewhere along the road of life, many of us are encouraged to dampen our fanciful and playful tendencies in favour of adopting a more responsible, productive and practical mindset. (Maybe this isn't your experience, but having spent many years both studying to be and practicing as an accountant, maybe things got a bit out of balance for me.)

I even think the whole extreme minimalist movement has played a role in fostering this mindset. Taking inventory of your belongings and adopting strict wardrobe rules sometimes doesn't leave a lot of room for fun, flexibility and creativity. I think the key is to find a way to allow beauty and practicality to gently dance together.

Give yourself permission to seek beauty in life (guilt free)! Although practical choices make sense in a number of situations, allow yourself to follow your heart when it comes to creating a home environment that feels welcoming and complements your personal style. Yes, the white couch sounds like a terrible idea, but if you think you can pull it off, (choosing a washable slip cover style, tending to stains regularly) then go for it. You will certainly get more "use" out of the bouquet of carnations, but why not choose the delicate white tulips instead? Your new centerpiece might not last as long, but since you prefer the quiet elegance of the later, go ahead and indulge.

## Seek Out the Pretty and Practical

One of my favorite quotes on the topic of home life is by William Morris. He wisely stated, "Have nothing in your house that you do not know to be useful, or believe to be beautiful." I keep this tidbit of wisdom in mind when bringing new things into my home, or deciding whether it is time to bid an item farewell.

The best case scenario, however, is when you are able to welcome an object into your home that ticks off *both* criteria. We all have a need for strictly utilitarian objects in our lives. These are items that serve specific purposes, but are not likely on display in our homes. We are, however, still going to interact with them, so why not make that experience as pleasant as possible? Anytime you need to acquire something new, aim to seek out the most attractive option available, without giving up on function (and staying within your budget, of course).

Even workhorse type objects in your home can have an elevated feel to them. When choosing a hammer for the tool kit, why not select the one with the natural wooden handle over the synthetic one? It will feel nicer to hold in your hand, and is frankly prettier to look at!

I recently decided to upgrade my kitchen compost bin. I switched out the drab green one issued by the municipality and opted for a vintage enamelware pot instead. What would I rather have staring me in the face on the kitchen counter, a shabby chic flea market find, or a crappy plastic container? This was not a difficult decision!

Of course, this doesn't just apply to your household belongings! It's worthwhile to adopt this principle in all areas of your life. (This might sound harsh, but life is too short to adorn your body in that boring and drab pair of tattered nude panties. Please see chapter 13 of my book, *Elevate Your Personal Style* for further discussion on this topic!)

## Think Beyond Society's Default Setting

There are so many objects we bring into our lives with very little thought or consideration. We often just reach for the default choice that is presented to us. Again, I don't mean to sound harsh or judgmental, but a lot of this "stuff" is unattractive, junky crap! Our homes are supposed to serve as restful and peaceful places to seek refuge from the outside world. Why then do we clutter them up with all this stuff that detracts from the beauty of our surroundings?

The first thing that pops in my head when I think of ugly junk is the plethora of plastic children's toys on the market! If you are a parent, I'm sure you are well acquainted with these garish objects littering the floor of your living room.

We had our first son shortly after we built our home, and it wasn't long before I knew I wanted to take a different approach when it came to providing him with toys and play spaces. I recoiled at the thought of a pile of junky toys occupying valuable space in my living room, and detracting from the aesthetically pleasing home environment my husband and I had proudly created.

My research on natural parenting lead me to the Walford and Montessori schools of thought. (If you have little ones in your life, I highly recommend looking into these approaches to early childhood education.) I realized that a child's environment and playthings deserve the same attention, care and aesthetic considerations that we adults grant ourselves. Instead of filling the toybox with mainstream options, I started sourcing natural, open-ended toys that were beautiful to touch, look at, and play with. In many instances, I made the toys myself, so each one felt like a miniature work of art. As I mentioned in chapter 1, I learned how to knit so I could create woolly playthings for my kids. I also took up some very simple woodworking and made animal figurines and tree branch blocks. I discovered that toys and child-friendly spaces can actually *enhance* a home's décor, as opposed to detract from it.

I don't want to give you the unrealistic impression that I don't have anything boring and ugly in my life. (Keep in mind, I am an everyday woman!) I definitely go the practical route on many occasions. My puppy Junior's dog crate is your standard, run of the mill plastic box. It's easy to clean and durable, which are priorities in this case. I don't especially like the look of it, but it's not a big deal. Also, please don't think my kids only played with wooden blocks and cloth dolls! I specifically remember Santa dropping a talking Buzz Lightyear down the chimney one year.

The idea is not to seek perfection, but to elevate your surroundings with as much beauty as possible.

## Make an Extra Effort

Sometimes, choosing beauty means spending a little extra time and effort, but not necessarily more money. When you are in need of something new in your home, it's worth considering all the alternatives, instead of just those that are convenient and widely available.

In my book, *Elevate the Everyday,* I have a chapter titled "Think Outside the Big Box When Shopping". In it I discuss my passion for sleuthing out treasures on the second-hand market. I purchase a ton of used clothing, and this is my favorite secret weapon for elevating my personal style. I also draw on the second-hand mindset when shopping for household products and furniture.

Shopping at a store like IKEA is easy when you are in need of inexpensive furniture (although I tend to find their warehouses incredibly irritating and frustrating to navigate). While I admit that some of their stuff is attractive, and I certainly have the odd piece in my home, a lot of it is really poor quality that won't stand the test of time. I'm thinking of their cheap pressboard furniture that disintegrates immediately upon contact with water (as one spilled bedside glass of water revealed in our household).

Both my kids have antique pine dressers that I picked up for $100-$125; less than the price of many of the pressboard versions! These dressers are handmade, solid wood and have a warm patina that only comes from authentic wear and time. Antiques might not be your style, but people are always selling furniture at discounted prices that is as good as new. You may be able to snag a higher quality option with a reasonable price tag.

You don't necessarily have to spend your weekends patiently sifting through dusty antique shops to access these types of goods. When it comes to online shopping, pretty much *everything* is available with the click of the mouse. My favorite place to pick up small and charming decorative items is Etsy. I purchased a set of vintage brass planters (again with swoon-worthy patina) that have so much more character than the store bought versions. My kitchen compost bin also came from Etsy, as well as a set of milk glass vases I use to store my makeup brushes and toothpaste.

Thinking outside the big box truly is a wonderful way to add unique items to your home that have more character and charisma. Next time you are in need of something new, try a little treasure hunting before jumping at the first item on the store shelf.

## Let Things Go Without Guilt

When my husband and I got married, we received many sets of stoneware as wedding gifts. Each set included a dinner plate, salad plate, cereal bowl and mug. I selected this particular pattern because it was sturdy, great for everyday use, and neutral in color. (There's that practical accountant in me shining through!) We've gotten a lot of use out of the bowls and plates, and I still love and use them daily. The mugs were another matter. I didn't particularly like the look or feel of them, and for years they collected dust on the top shelf of a kitchen cupboard. I didn't *love* them, and I clearly didn't *need* them. I own a gorgeous and eclectic collection of handmade pottery mugs. Many of them were made by my cousin and each one is unique. I enjoy the process of selecting a new one each day when brewing my tea. They elevate my morning routine!

One day I finally asked myself why I was hanging on to those plain, dusty mugs on the top shelf. The truth was, the practical side of me felt guilty by the thought of breaking up a set! Could the mugs make it on their own in the world without the rest of their matching family? I eventually realized I was being silly, and decided to purge them from my life.

Do you have idle objects hanging around your home, taking up mental and physical space? If they aren't beautiful or useful, (thank you Mr. Morris for this reminder) then maybe it's time to reassess and release them into the universe. One woman's trash is another woman's treasure. They are probably better off going to a loving home where they will be used and appreciated. Let them go guilt free!

## ELEVATING ACTIONS AND INSPIRATION

- Give yourself permission to make beauty a priority in life. It's perfectly acceptable to follow your heart on occasion, even when that means choosing the "impractical". Allow yourself to indulge in beautiful things for the sheer joy of it. Just because something is high-maintenance, delicate or trendy doesn't mean it's not worth bringing into your home.

- Look for opportunities where beauty and function-ality co-exist. When it comes to acquiring utilitarian objects for your home, seek out the most attractive option available. It's always a win-win situation when you find something that is both pretty *and* practical.

- Snap yourself out of default mode. Just because everyone else is shopping at big box stores, and filling their homes with standard issue objects, doesn't mean you have to. If you cringe at the thought of littering your home with cheap, junky objects, seek out more attractive alternatives. They *do* exist!

- Consider shopping the second-hand market for furniture and decorative objects. Antique and vintage items often have more charm and character than their new counterparts. You usually get more bang for your buck by acquiring a better quality item for the same price (or less!)

- You don't need to spend your weekends driving the back roads and hitting up antique shops (unless of course you want to!) Sourcing antique and vintage products is easier than ever, as they are readily available online. Etsy is a wonderful source for unique handmade and vintage items that will add warmth and personality to your living space.

- Let go of those items in your home you genuinely dislike without guilt. They are better off being appreciated and enjoyed by someone else, than collecting dust and taking up valuable space in your cupboards.

# 3

# ADOPT A VACATION
# STATE OF MIND

A s a young couple, my husband and I had grand
plans and dreams about the life we wanted to
create together. A big part of our vision centered
around our fantasy version of an ideal homelife.

We lived in some very tiny apartments for a number
of years, while we skimped, saved and searched for a property to plant our roots. We dreamed of designing and
building a home that embraced the spirit of a seaside,
cottage lifestyle.

We were extremely fortunate to find an ocean view
property just thirty minutes from our downtown office
jobs. (This is/was one of the perks of living in a place like
Nova Scotia...although real estate prices have skyrocketed
in recent years.) We then set to work drawing up house
plans that would *perfectly* suit our vision of the *perfect*

cottage life. (You probably guessed that it didn't take us long to learn that such a *perfect* life does not exist!)

In an effort to immerse ourselves in inspiration, we rented a small oceanside retreat for a few days; design books and graph paper in tow. "Puddingpan Cottage" was a mere three hundred square feet, and was the perfect location to absorb the essence of cottage life. We spent our days sketching, planning, dreaming and appreciating the simple, slow paced atmosphere of our surroundings. We came home with our final draft to send off to the home designer, pleased as punch with ourselves. How clever we felt! We were certain we had come up with the secret to a peaceful, happy life; make your home the cottage, and live the cottage-life year round!

Of course, we were young and naïve back then. We had no idea what was in store for us, and what the pressures of careers, parenting and marriage would throw our way. *Escaping* to the cottage life is easier said than done when faced with the grind of reality.

That being said, our home has remained the focal point of our lives as a family. It is the one place we can all come together at the end of the day. It is our safe haven and a place of refuge from the stressors of the outside world.

Despite the reality check that adulthood has given me, I still strive to seek ways to live a cottage lifestyle and adopt a *vacation state of mind*. I'm not saying I walk around pretending to be on a holiday, but rather I aim to seek out small opportunities to tap into a vacation mindset, allowing for moments in my day to relax and let go.

It's actually a fun challenge to identify snippets of time where you can set yourself free on vacation. If you are lucky, you might be able to treat yourself to a weekend getaway! My goal, however, it to look for ways to incorporate the spirit of vacation into my day-to-day life at home. My mini vacations might take place on a Friday night, a Sunday afternoon, or during one delicious hour to myself mid-day.

## Capture the Essence of Vacation

Have you ever sat back and contemplated exactly *how* you *feel* when you are on vacation? Maybe you were too busy relaxing and enjoying the sights to take notice. That's not a bad thing! I've done some research on the matter, so I'd love to share my thoughts with you.

I decided to write this chapter while on holiday at the family cottage. (Writing never feels like work, so it pairs perfectly with the vacation state of mind!) Every summer we retreat to the cottage owned on my mother's side. As a child, I spent many days walking these shores, and revisiting each year invokes a nostalgic sense of coming home inside me. This is a place to truly slow down, unwind and do nothing. We get to fall asleep to the sound of lapping waves, and exfoliate our skin all night in our sand-filled sheets. I knew it would serve as the perfect place to conduct my "study".

Being immersed in a real vacation allowed me to record, study, contemplate, analyse and draw conclusions on all the key aspects of the vacation state of mind. I was able to capture my thoughts and feelings in real time. The plan was to bottle up the essence of vacation, and bring it home, along with my treasures of sea glass and sea shells. I wondered… could I find a way to pull the cork out of the bottle and pour myself a taste of vacation whenever it suited me?

May I now present to you the results of my study? I tried to identify what aspects of vacation make the atmosphere special, relaxing, free and fun. Here's what I came up with:

- The days feel like a blank canvas. There is no set agenda for the day.
- Mornings unfold at a leisurely and unhurried pace.
- I feel disconnected from the world, and don't feel the need to get a news update.
- I enjoy having a tiny, coordinated selection of clothes that mix and match together easily. Life feels low maintenance when I open the closet. With limited choices, decision making is effortless.

- My small collection of beauty products I packed is all I need to feel pretty and pulled-together. There is no need to rummage through drawers. It's all right here in my cosmetic bag.

- I don't miss my belongings back home. I'm making out just fine with the contents of my single suitcase.

- The cottage feels so airy and clutter free. It's a soothing space to spend time in.

- As an introvert, I enjoy the moments of anonymity while on vacation. I don't feel the need to stop and chat with everyone I encounter. A pleasant hello in passing is all that is required.

- Naps are always a good idea.

- Simple, no-fuss meals feel just as nourishing and tasty as their more elaborate counterparts. I don't need anything complicated to keep me happy and satiated.

Now it's your turn. I realize I'm dropping this in your lap, and if you aren't reading this book on vacation, it might be a bit more challenging to come up with your own list off the top of your head. You can still sit back and reminisce about the best vacation you ever had! Identify a list of all the aspects (big and small) that made it feel delicious and dreamy.

I also recognize that we might not share the same vision of a dream vacation. Maybe you yearn for something that offers more excitement and energy. Be sure to consider your own personal preferences when drafting your description of a vacation state of mind.

## Seek Opportunity and Take Action

Now that we've identified the key components that make a vacation so pleasurable, it's time to get creative! While most of us can't embark on a never-ending holiday, (even retirees have demands, obligations and commitments) we can seek to elevate moments of each day by unbottling the essence of vacation when we need it most.

I'm going to walk through a list of ideas I came up with that suit my personal lifestyle. Again, this is a *personal* list. Borrow some of my thoughts, and feel free to sprinkle in your own.

## Seek Blank Canvas Moments

Sit up and take notice when your schedule offers a blank canvas moment. Although you might not be free to do as you wish all day, that doesn't mean you can't spare an afternoon, evening, or even an hour to fill as you desire. Instead of squandering away free time mindlessly on your phone, choose to deliberately paint your canvas. How would you most like to spend an hour to yourself at home? Would you lock the bathroom door and escape into a warm bath? Would you put your feet up and read that riveting novel?

## Rise Before the Sun

How could you make your mornings feels less hectic? What could you do to give them an easy, breezy vacation vibe? I choose to get up really early so I have tons of time to myself before I need to rustle the kids into action. Not only do I have time to exercise, but I also have time to chat with my husband and sip my tea slowly.

Another option is to take care of administrative duties the night before. Pack lunches, set out the breakfast supplies, lay out your outfit for the next day, and check the kids' homework. Moving this work ahead will free up more time in the morning. Even an extra few minutes makes a difference!

## Choose Your News

Whenever I'm on vacation, I naturally feel less connected to the world. I usually make a conscious effort to stay off the news apps. The stories are 99% depressing, and are usually the same terrible tale being told on repeat day after day.

I'm not suggesting we tuck our heads in the sand and ignore important world issues. While it's lovely to completely pull the plug during vacation, this is not realistic in daily life. It's helpful to look for ways to loosen your grip on the "need to know" mindset. This past year I chose to back off on world news, and focus on the local and provincial news. The local news affected my day-to-day life. With kids in school and a pandemic evolving, I needed to stay informed of the situation in our area. Beyond that, I let days pass before tuning into the rest of the world.

## Pack for the Month

There is something freeing about being able to fit everything you need into a single tiny suitcase. (This was not the case for the rest of my family who packed three mountain bikes, three surfboards and all related gear for our one week trip to the beach.) We always get by just fine with a limited selection of clothing and cosmetics. Ironically, when we return home, we can't imagine living without our extensive collection of belongings. I'll dive into this topic in greater depth in chapter 8, (clutter definitely deserves its own chapter) but for now I want to plant the seed that we can all live with less.

Why not set up your closet or bathroom vanity as if you were on a month-long holiday? Carefully "pack" what you need for the month and tuck away the rest in storage or out of sight. Take note of how you feel as your pretend getaway unfolds. Did you miss the variety and selection? Did you enjoy having fewer choices? Did decision making feel lighter? We will revisit these notes in chapter 8 so hang on to them!

# Embrace a Clean Aesthetic

Coming home from the cottage always inspires me to revisit my need for so many belongings. Our cottage is shared by four families, so it's really not possible for everyone to fill it with their own "stuff". The families have a system in place to keep personal belongings in the main living area to a minimum. (Everyone is designated a small storage area.) As a result, the cottage has a very clean, carefree and spacious aesthetic. It offers the perfect atmosphere to clear your mind and unwind. In my travels, I've noticed that many of the Airbnb's we've rented emit this same vibe.

How can we add a touch of that open, airy vacation ambiance to our homes? Clearing off all surfaces of clutter is a good first step. (Again, I zone in on clutter in detail in chapter 8). Start by removing all the contents from the kitchen counter, the coffee table, the dining room table and your bedside table. Now add back just a few small decorative or utilitarian pieces, pretending you are setting up the scene for a guest!

# Seek Out Anonymity

I am very much an introvert. Some people associate this with being antisocial, but that's actually a misconception. I genuinely enjoy socializing, (usually in small, intimate settings) but there are times I just want to be alone with my thoughts.

Being on vacation allows you to meander around as you please, incognito. You *become* that mysterious woman walking down the beach, drinking coffee on the terrace, or reading alone under the palm tree. Although I love catching up with neighbours, sometimes it's nice to go on my merry way, without feeling the need to stop and chat (or gossip!) When on holiday, you might exchange pleasantries with strangers, but there is no need to take it any further than that. It's kind of a refreshing break!

I was forced to adopt the anonymity approach recently while training my dog Coco. He is a reactive dog. (This is a nice way of saying that he barks at everyone he crosses paths with.) The training techniques were difficult to implement when encountering people I knew personally. Basically, I had to respect his comfort zone, (which involved a very wide girth). Stopping to chat with my neighbour pushing a baby carriage was not an option. I found it easier and more pleasant to hop in the car and drive to an area of town I didn't know anyone. I still said hello to passersby, but was able to walk Coco through the training process at a pace that better suited him. (He's made so much progress!)

If you crave a little mystery in your life at home as I do, ask yourself how you might achieve a lower profile on occasion. Instead of taking your daily walk around your own neighbourhood, mix it up and explore a nearby community. You will be less likely to bump into someone you know! Again, this might sound antisocial to some, but I prefer to view it as self-loving. There is no shame in taking a vacation from socializing!

## Surrender to Naps

No one has ever regretted a nap. Need I say more? Naps seem to come naturally and innocently on vacation. We give ourselves guilt-free permission to set that book aside and snooze for a spell. And while the unhurried pace of vacation allows for this, seeking out opportunities to do the same during your "regular" life back home is probably more important.

Make a commitment to yourself to nap when you need or want to! If it's Sunday afternoon, and you have a zillion things to accomplish before a new week begins, don't fight that urge to snuggle up on the couch for a restful pause. A nourishing nap will leave you feeling refreshed, and will likely give you that boost of energy you need to tackle your to-do list.

I regularly nap in my vehicle while waiting for my kids at one of their activities. (I've even been known to bring along a pillow and blanket!)

## Dine Vacation Style

I'm not sure that anyone associates vacation with toiling in the kitchen (unless perhaps you are on a food tour in Italy!) Because I handle most of the cooking in our household, stepping away from this task on occasion feels luxurious. Even if cooking is one of your passions, we all need a break from the kitchen now and then.

Dining out is a common treat on holiday, but some of my best vacation meals have been casual dine-in affairs. I love picking up a few simple ingredients and creating a spontaneous tapas-style meal. Suggestions for a shopping list include fresh baguettes, antipasto, local fruit, olives, humus, cheese, crudités…use your imagination!

What these casual vacation meals teach me is that simple, easy meals can feel just as satisfying and indulgent as more elaborate options.

Designate one night of the week to dine vacation style! Offer a selection of "tastings" and pretend you are sitting on a French stone terrace, indulging in the day's fresh market finds.

Give yourself a break by designating one night a week or month for take-out. Treat yourself to something nicer than a greasy pizza. These days, pretty much every food establishment is set up for takeaway, so the options are limitless.

Switch up roles and delegate the cooking to your partner or children. Meal kits are great for teens and budding chefs. They allow children to feel independent in the kitchen without Mom or Dad hovering close by.

# ELEVATING ACTIONS AND INSPIRATION

- Home is meant to be a place to rest, relax, unplug and unwind. It serves as an escape from the outside world and provides a space to both recharge our batteries ,and connect with those we love the most.

- Sit back and reminisce about some of your favorite vacations in the past. Make a list of all the aspects of these getaways that appealed to you. Try to capture the essence of what the vacation state of mind means to *you*!

- Identify blank canvas moments in your day-to-day life. Make the most of this free time by intentionally doing something that brings you joy, instead of letting it mindlessly slip away.

- Consider getting up earlier each day to allow mornings to flow at a less hectic pace.

- Move as many morning tasks to the night before. Having the lunches packed and your clothes laid out will help free up some time.

- Taking the weight of the world off your shoulders can do wonders for reducing stress. Unplugging from the news regularly is a great approach. At times, however, you do need to know what's going on around you. Choose your news wisely and focus on the local news that is relevant to your life. Bypass the rest of the dismal stories!

- Try "packing" for your life at home! Carefully choose a selection of clothing and cosmetics to get you through the next couple of weeks or months. Tuck away all the excess, out of sight if possible. Make note of how living with less made you feel.

- Experiment with the concept of setting your home up as if you were a guest. Would the coffee table be cluttered with dirty mugs and tattered magazines? Create a clean, breezy aesthetic that allows your mind to feel calm and in holiday mode.

- Seek out anonymity when you feel the need to step back from the social scene of daily life. Explore outside your neighbourhood and cruise around in disguise for the day.

- Unapologetically incorporate naps into your regular life. Allowing yourself a rest when you need it will make you more efficient and productive. (Hint: blank canvas moments make perfect nap opportunities!)

- Regularly schedule vacation-style meals into your life at home. Treat yourself to a special night out or an elevated take-out option. Delegate the cooking to your partner or kids. Create a casual appetizer-style meal that's simple to pull together, yet very tasty.

# 4

# SET YOURSELF UP FOR SUCCESS

After all this talk of vacation, magic and fairies, it feels appropriate to come back to earth for a bit of a reality check. While I love sprinkling my homelife with beauty and peaceful moments of relaxation, there inevitably comes a time when I feel a burning desire to *get sh!t done*. (If you read my book *Elevate the Everyday*, you will know that I am working on scrubbing my potty mouth. That being said, there is no other expression that more accurately describes how I feel when I enter the zone of productivity).

I was one of those people who couldn't start studying for an exam until my dorm room was in perfect order. Back then, cleaning up my pig pen was no small feat. I let a lot of areas in my life slide during my university years. I might have been a stellar student, but I definitely got a failing grade when it came to health habits and cleanliness.

I think maybe we all need to go through this kind of phase in life. Perhaps growing sick of our own slovenly habits allows us to mature into better adults (at least this is what I choose to believe when I walk pass my children's bedrooms).

My self-imposed "clean desk rule" during exam time was definitely a procrastination tool! I do, however, believe that my inability to focus amid the clutter was deeply rooted in my DNA. I was a very organized and tidy child, so I eventually circled back to my instinctive need for cleanliness and order in early adulthood. I think most people are most productive when they are in an orderly environment, free of distraction (even if they don't want to admit it).

Today I adopt a somewhat balanced approach to housekeeping, however, there is *one* area of my house that I am a stickler about—my home "office". It's actually the loft area over our garage, and is really more of a multi-purpose room. Although it's where my desktop is set up, it also serves as a TV room, guest room and my husband's meditation nook. It gets a lot of use!

Many people were forced to get creative with their living spaces during the pandemic. While working from home, people needed to find a way to accomplish employment, academic and personal tasks all under one roof. I'm guessing many had less than ideal setups, and struggled to draw a firm line between business and personal activities.

While I don't have a conventional job, I do spend a fair amount of time at my desk. This is my fourth book in just over a year, so I've obviously clocked many hours tapping on my keyboard! I also handle the accounting for my husband's professional corporation, as well as our personal household expenses.

Whether you work from home every day, on occasion, or not at all, we all have a need for an at-home workspace. A lot of personal tasks in life require focus and attention. Having the optimal setup will allow you to work more efficiently, and perhaps with greater enjoyment!

## Make it Pretty

Who says a workspace has to be sterile and boring? I was employed at an accounting firm for over a decade, so I'm well aware of life in the corporate cubicle. The great thing about a home office or workspace is that you have free reign over the set up and decorating! Why not take the opportunity to infuse it with your own signature style?

I have found that the nicer my surroundings, the more likely I'm willing to sit at my desk and plough through something yucky. If I'm going to be working on an unpleasant task, (my annual update of Canadian income tax rules) I'd rather do it surrounded by beauty and inspiration. Yes, I have been known to do accounting by candlelight! When I am focused on a more blissful task, (writing my books) my creative juices flow more freely in the presence of my pretty things.

If you aren't happy with your workspace, maybe it's time to redecorate! You don't need to paint the walls or buy new furniture to do this. Instead, you can just add a few special touches that one might not normally associate with an office environment.

Being surrounded by a mess of wires and papers will have you feeling defeated before you even sit down to work. The first step, of course, will be to clear the clutter. Once you have a clean desk, you can start to add tidbits of inspiration! Choose objects you love and connect with, and that ignite excitement and drive inside you.

I thought it would be fun to give you a visual of what my own writing/accounting desk looks like. I love this little nook so much, that I look forward to my time here each day.

My desk is actually an old work bench I found on the side of the road. I'm pretty sure it was in someone's garage! I took it home and refinished the top. It suits my rustic, natural style and is the perfect height. I have an Apple iMac that sits in the center of my desk. To the left is an essential oil diffuser that I run occasionally. To my right, I always create a small display of objects that inspire and motivate me. This is an evolving space. Its contents rotate depending on my mood and what I'm working on. Today it is a bouquet of beach roses in a mason jar, a seashell I picked up during my last trip to the beach, and a lavender scented candle. (Interestingly, this exact flower arrangement turned up on the cover of this book!) Next to my keyboard is an antique glass tumbler filled with sharp pencils and pretty pens. I purchased an adorable pink mousepad on Etsy. It showcases a French-girl inspired print of the Eiffel tower, French bulldogs and ballet flat shoes. It probably goes without saying, but there is a stack of journals on hand filled with notes and lists that I refer to regularly. There is also usually a steaming cup of tea nearby in one of my favorite mugs. Last but not least, I positioned a cuddly dog bed under my desk, the perfect spot for my faithful "helpers" to hang out while I work. (I forgot to mention the bag of dog treats next to my pencils.)

My desk strikes the perfect balance, as my set up allows me to tap into both my creative and productive sides. It is clutter free, but is enhanced with a few key objects that bring me joy. Have fun creating your own inspiring spot. Fill it with all your favorite things and elevate the experience of getting sh!t done!

## Set the Mood With Music

In addition to prettying up your space, you can also set the mood with music. It's really a personal preference. Some people enjoy background music while they are working, and some prefer complete silence.

I take a mixed bag approach. When I'm doing something that involves numbers, I require total peace and quiet. When I'm writing, I play soft background music. I wrote all twenty two chapters of *Elevate the Everyday* to the same song on repeat! I'm not sure about the science behind what was going on in my brain, but as soon as I turned on this particular tune, the words just flowed! Interestingly, the song is called *Motion* by Peter Sandberg. I think it subconsciously made me feel like I had set myself in motion towards my goal of writing a book! I really enjoy a lot of Peter's music and have branched out to include other songs of his on my writing soundtrack. If you like calming music with a chill vibe, I encourage you to check him out.

If you haven't worked to music before, it's worth giving it a try to see if it impacts your concentration and productivity. There has actually been a lot of research done on this topic, so you can investigate what genres of music have been proven to have the most positive results. My husband swears by classical music. He often wears his headphones at work if there is something pressing he needs to focus on. I've tried to encourage my children to play concentration music while doing homework, but they absolutely hate it. To each his own I guess!

# Personalize Your Paper Products

The family of my best friend growing up owned a printing business. I still feel a sense of nostalgia imagining being greeted by the strong smell of ink when we popped into the shop after school. The most beloved gift I ever received from her was a set of personalized stationery for my sweet sixteenth birthday. I was a big letter writer back then, (when snail mail was actually still a form of communication) and was absolutely tickled to see my name and address officially printed on the top of the page. I still have a few sheets of this writing paper left, along with the matching envelopes tucked away in a memorabilia box. It was a heavyweight cream stock with a rough bottom edge, deep burgundy lettering, and to top it off, an elegant little image of a pig (my signature back then as I was a collector of all things piggy related!) Crafting sentences on that special paper added a more serious, official and important tone to my words. I liked the way it felt!

I realize the world is going paperless, but it doesn't mean *you* have to as well. I still put pen to paper when preparing a to-do list, and I don't think I could ever give up pretty journals and diaries. To add a little sparkle to my list of chores, I recently ordered a set of personalized note pads. Somehow, seeing my name professionally printed at the top of a piece of paper still makes me feel more important! I also did up a set of corresponding journals and pens to match. It's just more fun to work with pretty supplies, so why not allow yourself this small pleasure?

These days, customizing anything from mugs, to calendars to thank-you cards is accessible to everyone. You don't need to be a graphic designer as there are so many websites out there that offer this service at very reasonable prices. You can use the templates they provide and modify them with your name, or you can start from scratch and download your own images and lettering as I did. (I used the custom artwork I commissioned for my books.)

## Limit Distractions

Limiting distractions in the home environment is tough, and I'm not going to pretend that I have a magical solution to this problem. I'm guessing kids top the list as the number one distraction for most people. I can relate!

When I decided to write my first book, we just happened to be smack in the middle of the first worldwide pandemic lockdown. Our schools were closed, and so the whole family was home together for months. We have a decent-sized house, but for some reason, it still felt like I couldn't escape the company of others. The main issue was the fact that my home office shared the space with the one and only TV in the house. When my computer finally freed up from homeschooling, the kids plunked in front of the TV. The TV was inconveniently situated right beside the very space I planned to spend the afternoon in quiet solitude, recording my thoughts. It was not an ideal situation!

We had always been a one TV household, as it was something I felt very strongly about…until the day I didn't! We purchased another television for the kids and set it up in the basement. (I'll fill you in on the great story behind this move in chapter 7.) Loosening my grip and letting go of my rigid opinions on home electronics set me free! I had the space to myself again, and haven't stopped writing since!

My kids are *sort of* old enough to follow instructions when I post a "Do Not Disturb" sign. Of course, most things that come up for them are of an urgent nature (hunger), so they often find an excuse to interrupt me. That being said, posting a sign on my office door does divert them on occasion, which is better than nothing. I'm guessing this approach would have zero impact on toddlers or pets!

Rearranging furniture and posting signs are just a couple of suggestions that I understand might not be options for everyone. The fact that we had the basement available certainly helped solve my problem. I realize everyone might not have the luxury of space. I think the key takeaway here is to try to think outside the box and look at all options available to limit distraction. My sister actually set up her home office in her son's bedroom. Since he was down in the rec room most of day, this quiet little corner of their home offered the perfect hideaway.

## Close Shop

When the workday is done, I like to walk through an informal process of "closing shop". Tidying up the space to prepare it for the following day means you can hit the ground running next time you sit down to work. I don't like being greeted by a cluttered and messy desk at the start of a fresh day, so I take a few moments to tidy up any loose ends, organize my papers and save my work!

One habit I've carried over from my days at the accounting firm is to end each day with a list. Before I leave my desk, I roughly plan out my tasks for the following day. I always list them based on priority, with the most urgent matters at the top. This allows me to walk away from my desk and switch gears from work mode to home mode. Recording the list of reminders allows me to download my thoughts, and prevents me from circling back to them when I'm supposed to be relaxing and enjoying an evening off. If I know they are written down, then I can forget about them in the moment.

# ELEVATING ACTIONS AND INSPIRATION

- A home workspace is an important part of most households. Having it set up in an organized and attractive fashion allows you to work more efficiently, productively and with greater enjoyment.
- The first order of business is to clear the clutter from your desk! Aim to create a blank canvas that you can then personalize and beautify to your liking.
- Have fun adding special and inspiring touches to your workspace that will motivate you to tackle your objectives. Candles, flowers, pretty postcards, picture books and special mementos all make great decorative additions!
- Consider setting the mood with music! Certain types of music have been proven scientifically to increase concentration. Experiment with different options to see if there is something that works for you.
- If you prefer to work in peace and quiet, consider investing in a pair of noise-cancelling headphones.
- Take an extra step in the personalization process and include a few custom-made products into your stationery collection. This is just plain fun! Your to-do list will most definitely be elevated by pretty paper.
- Limit distractions as much as possible when working. Consider your family situation and space restrictions

and brainstorm a list of flexible solutions that could limit the number of interruptions in your day.

- At the end of your workday, take the time to close up shop and tie up any loose ends. Tidy up your space so it feels fresh and organized the next time you sit down to work. Make a to-do list so you hit the ground running the next day.

# 5

# ELEVATE YOUR STYLE
# AT HOME

I wrote a whole book about elevating your personal style, so it might not be a surprise that I can't stop myself from voicing my opinion on the matter yet again. In fact, I'm so passionate about the issue of dress, and how it impacts day-to-day life, that it has been a topic of discussion in all four of my books. I even found a way to weave it into *Elevate Your Health,* because yes, what you wear while sweating matters! This time around, however, I'd like to focus on the matter of elevating your personal style specifically while living your life at *home.*

You might think what you wear while hiding inside your cave is of little consequence, but please hear me out. What you wear impacts how you feel, whether you are out running errands, in a meeting at the office, cooking dinner for your family, or snuggled up on the couch with a good book and a cup of tea. Whether you are under the scrutiny of the public eye is really quite irrelevant, because you are dressing first and foremost for yourself!

Perhaps this concept is easier for me to get my head around, because I have lived on both ends of the spectrum. I have a lot of experience (in other words failures) to draw wisdom from.

When I worked in a professional setting as an accountant, I used to dress up in suits and pearls. As soon as I left the corporate world to raise my children, things went downhill pretty quickly! Jeans, yoga pants, t-shirts (usually the kind you get for free) and sweatshirts represented the bulk of my mom-duty uniform. I pretty much put zero effort into my appearance and it showed, not just physically, but mentally as well.

The days at home with two needy toddlers were long. Although I was blissfully in love with my sons, I wasn't feeling the same deep affection for myself. To be honest, I felt and looked like crap. There were countless days where I never got around to a shower or a change of wardrobe (meaning I wore my pajamas all day). My uninspiring, sloppy dressing impacted my mood, my energy levels, and most of all, my self-esteem.

I've come a long way since those frazzled days of early motherhood. My book, *Elevate Your Personal Style,* chronicles my journey to improve both my appearance and my sense of self-worth. To sum things up, I eventually realized that ignoring my own needs and desires was dragging me down. Once I started putting more care and attention into how I dressed and presented myself each day, I not only started to carry myself with more confidence, I started to *feel* more confident.

We all care what others think of us, to some degree or another. This is just part of being human. This is most likely why we tend to put more care and attention into our appearance when going out in public. It's easy to let things slide at home when no one is looking. The truth is, at home you share company with the most important person in your life—you!

With this in mind, it's time to ask yourself, are you dressing to impress yourself? Is your home wardrobe in need of a shake up or upgrade?

## Define Your Days

I tend to categorize homelife activities into three main categories: *on-duty*, *off-duty* and *heavy-duty*. What you choose to wear at home will depend on which category your day (or part of your day) falls under.

Adjusting your attire based on your planned tasks and activities for the day will elevate your mood, no matter what you have on the agenda. You will feel your best when dressed appropriately, whether you are planning a day of relaxing self-care, or determined to cross every item off your to-do list.

Let's take a closer look at each category. As we go through them, think about how your current approach to homelife dressing compares to the vision we are about to walk through. Make style notes along the way, so you can tweak and adjust your sartorial selections next time you open your closet.

## Dress for On-Duty Mode

You shift into *on-duty mode* during those times of the day you are doing productive work around the home. You might be actively moving about your house, or sitting at a desk. (Particularly strenuous or messy jobs will come later when we discuss heavy-duty mode.)

On-duty mode includes activities such as cooking meals, performing employment duties, organizing household schedules and finances, caring for small children and light house cleaning.

Just as the state of our workspace impacts our productivity levels, so does the state of our dress. If you are wearing clothes that make you feel frumpy, frazzled and lazy, it's likely the energy you put into you daily to-do list will mirror your inner state.

Making a small effort each day to dress and groom for your role at home will elevate your mood, mindset *and* productivity. I'm not suggesting that you dress in formal business attire. I'm just recommending that you take the time to put together an outfit that makes you look and feel great. Take a few moments to style your hair attractively (baseball caps were my default), and freshen your face with some light makeup, if it suits your style. Add a finishing touch with a spritz of your favorite perfume and dash of sparkle. (My gold hoops are an everyday staple for me.)

My on-duty wardrobe is a collection of mostly casual clothes and includes everything from jeans and nice t-shirts, to pretty blouses, sweaters and dresses. It doesn't have to be formal or dressy to have an elevated vibe.

Trust me, I speak from experience, making these small efforts each day can work wonders. You may even feel that the fairy from chapter 1 waived her magic wand over you! When I feel and look pulled together, I sit taller at my desk, there is pep to my step when delivering laundry, and I become a master at manipulating the family schedule. I feel like the queen of my house!

## Dress for Off-Duty Mode

There is something decadent and delicious about *off-duty mode*. As I mentioned in chapter 3, viewing your home as a safe haven and refuge from the outside world allows you to unwind, reset and connect with the special people in your life. Many of life's simplest yet sweetest moments take place during off-duty mode.

Whether you work outside the home or not, it's important to allow yourself off-duty time each day. Slipping out of your work clothes and into your off-duty outfit is one way you can let go of the heaviness of the office or the daunting to-do list.

If you are retired or work from home for either employment or care-giving purposes, please resist the urge to consider your entire day off-duty. It's easy to slip into the mindset that because you are home, off-duty attire is the best choice.

Off-duty clothing should be comfortable, cozy and allow for free movement. Let me point out that comfortable doesn't necessarily mean sloppy! Don't you still want to look and feel good about yourself when you are cuddling with your lover or reading a juicy novel on the couch?

Considering your loungewear as an important part of your wardrobe allows you to make it the priority that it is. You don't need a large collection of loungewear, but I suggest you have pieces that you love and that make you feel good inside and out. I'm thinking those sloppy ill-fitting gym pants, pilled and faded yoga pants, and old t-shirts from your youth probably won't provide the elevated air you are looking for!

My personal loungewear collection consists mostly of menswear-style silk pajamas. They are incredibly comfortable, but also quite elegant looking. I also have a pair of cashmere leggings that are perfect for a cold winter's day by the woodstove. Cashmere sweaters make up a huge part of my regular wardrobe. When they start to approach the end of their life, I retire them to my off-duty wardrobe. Since they are beautiful, cozy, soft and sexy, they add an elevated feel to my lounging!

I'm a huge fan of Yonka skincare products, and have been using them for years! I love their clean and natural fragrance. Using them each day adds a hint of the authentic spa experience to my at-home beauty routine.

Last Christmas, my favorite spa was selling Yonka robes. I immediately fell in love with them and picked one up as a gift for my mother. Who wouldn't want to bring the spa home with them? As soon as I got home, I tried it on…and I never took it off. (Sorry Mom, hopefully they bring them in again this year so I can follow through on my gift.) It's pristine white, plush, and cozy and each time I wear it, I feel enveloped in luxury. Whenever I really want to take off-duty mode to the next level, I pull on my spa robe. If you don't have one already, I highly recommend treating yourself to the thickest, coziest, softest bathrobe you can find!

# Dress for Heavy-Duty Mode

Heavy-duty mode doesn't equal unpleasant. In fact, many of my favorite activities fall under the heavy-duty category.

Heavy-duty activities include anything that is strenuous or messy. Exercising, gardening, heavy cleaning, painting, and yard work all fall into this category.

Obviously, you don't want to be wearing anything valuable or delicate while engaging in these types of activities. (I was once scolded by my husband for piling firewood in designer jeans!) This is where you actually get to pull out that old college t-shirt and ratty sweatpants and wear them with a purpose!

Scheduling messy activities into your day is a great approach to ensure you are dressed appropriately for the task at hand. I exercise first thing in the morning, so I tack on grimy jobs while I'm still wearing my workout clothes. I take advantage of the fact that I'm already sweaty and smelly, and jump at the opportunity to bring in a load of firewood, sweep out the dusty garage, or gather up the garbage and recycling for the curb.

I make use of my apron often, in situations I feel it provides enough protection. Cooking obviously falls into this category, but I might slip it on if I'm cleaning the bathroom or tucking a few pieces of firewood into the woodstove.

For really heavy-duty work, there is a *very special* item in my wardrobe that I've had for over seventeen years. It classifies as a true thrift store treasure! It's a mechanic's suit from the old provincial phone company and unbelievably, it fits my 5'3" frame perfectly! It was basically made for me.

It's probably the most versatile piece in my wardrobe, and I suspect I'll hang on to it forever. I've worn it to paint my entire house, refinish countless antiques, mow the lawn and till the garden. After getting caught in my expensive jeans at the woodpile, I now slip it over whatever I'm wearing when stacking firewood. It has even served as a Halloween costume on several occasions. At the risk of sounding silly, I'll admit that I wrote a short jingle about it. It's titled, *Got My Shop Suit* and yes, I belt it out every time I pull on this endearing piece.

Of course, I need to recommend you find your very own shop suit! If that sounds crazy, at least treat yourself to the cutest apron on the market, so you can elevate your dirty work!

# ELEVATING ACTIONS AND INSPIRATION

- Elevating your style at home and dressing appropriately for the task at hand can have a huge impact on your mood, mindset and productivity.

- There are three main modes of operation in daily homelife: on-duty, off-duty and heavy-duty. Coordinating your wardrobe with your mode will produce optimal results, whether you are achieving goals, or relaxing the day away.

- When operating in on-duty mode, choose outfits that make you feel pulled together and productive. They should be both attractive and comfortable, so you can go about your tasks with ease and confidence.

- Off-duty clothes should feel free and comforting. Choose items that allow you to relax and unwind, while still feeling good about yourself. Pretty loungewear, cozy pajamas and fresh fluffy robes make great choices.

- Save your grubbiest clothes for heavy-duty mode. Life is messy, and we all have hobbies and tasks that involve getting our hands dirty. Enjoy these jobs and play sessions without worrying about ruining your nice things.

- Look into acquiring your very own shop suit (seriously)! I'm almost thinking of designing my own version, complete with *The Elevated Everyday* logo!

# 6

# INVITE MOTHER NATURE
# IN FOR A VISIT

As much as I am a homebody, I'm also a nature lover. I'm just as comfortable outdoors as I am snuggled up behind the four walls of my home. As a child, we had a tall poplar tree in the backyard where I spent a good chunk of my time. I could often be found perched high on a branch, completely engrossed in my latest novel. I was just as happy resting on that tree branch as I would have been nestled in bed with a stack of fluffy pillows. This is probably one of the reasons I was nicknamed "Monkey" growing up! (I'll admit it wasn't as perfect and dreamy as it sounds. I did fall out of that tree and broke and dislocated my arm! It wasn't while reading, but while trying to re-enact a gymnastics move I had watched Mary Lou Retton pull off in her 1984 gold medal performance.)

Spending time in my comforting home environment and getting outside to enjoy nature are equally important to my mental health. I make sure to allocate time for each, no matter my schedule for the day. I like to compare this need to the simple and natural act of breathing. Inhaling and exhaling are equally important parts of the process, and both are required to sustain life. Getting out in nature allows me to inhale the beauty of the world around me and soak in energy from it. When it's time to come home to my peaceful refuge, I allow myself to exhale, relax and reset.

## Embrace Natural Materials

When it comes to home décor, it's no surprise that I am drawn to natural materials. I prefer a very natural aesthetic, so I enjoy surrounding myself with creations made by Mother Nature herself. I aim to marry my love of the outdoors and indoors. Inviting the beauty of the outside world into my home definitely elevates the atmosphere of my living space. Natural materials have a richness of character that can't be replicated by synthetics. Because they have a personal history and were once pulsing with life, it almost feels like natural objects carry a bit of a soul inside them (at least the romantic side of me likes to think so).

If your goal is to add warmth and character to your home, it's always worth reaching for the most natural and authentic option available (when your budget allows. Yes, the accountant in me feels the need to emphasize this point.)

Instead of opting for ceramic tile in my entryway, I chose natural slate. Because I only needed a small quantity, I purchased it at a discount flooring store. It ended up being the same price as ceramic, but because each tile is unique, this small floor space is oozing with character.

Take a few minutes to scan your current surroundings. What are your favorite objects that catch your eye and give you a pleasing boost? My guess is that they are likely items that feel real, unique and authentic, instead of "factory made". Why not look for ways to add a few more natural touches to your surroundings? Here is a list of some of my favorite objects in my home to get your own creative juices flowing:

- A richly hued antique leather chair
- Perfectly imperfect linen curtains hanging in my bathroom
- A sleek marble pastry board (I scavenged this from the side of the road!)
- My beach stone woodstove hearth
- A cozy cashmere throw
- A colorful woolen floor rug
- Sweetly scented beeswax candles
- Earthy handmade pottery bowls
- Antique wooden furniture
- An artfully woven basket
- A vintage hand-blown glass buoy

Certainly, any home furnishing store is going to have some of these items on hand. You can also check out your local antique and craft shops, or my favorite online source from chapter 2, Etsy.

## Go on a Scavenger Hunt

As pointed out in chapter 2, beautiful doesn't always equal expensive (although sometimes it certainly does!) Many of the items I use to decorate my home were free of charge, because I found them hiding in a tree, or peeking out of the sand.

Over the years, I have amassed a collection of treasured objects that I discovered on walks in the woods or beach-combing expeditions. I have an antique postal desk in my living room that I use to display them. It has a series of twenty small compartments (mail slots!) that lends itself perfectly to this use. My collection includes bird nests, sea shells, sea glass, fossils, feathers, dried seed pods and interesting stones. These one-of-a-kind treasures are priceless and add so much warmth and character to my home.

Next time you venture out on a nature walk or family hike, keep your eyes peeled! When you spot a pretty offering from Mother Nature, slip it in your pocket (but please never take home something that is in use, like a mother bird's nest of eggs). I have a friend who collects heart shaped rocks. She displays them on a window ledge in her kitchen, so each time she stands at the sink, she is reminded of her many special outings. This might be a fun challenging project to get your started!

## Use Your Green Thumb

Fresh flowers and plants obviously add instant beauty to any space. You don't need to break the bank to give your home a greenhouse vibe. Once again, there are lots of free options available in the botanical department.

So many houseplants are easy to propagate, so you can expand your inventory easily at no additional cost. Trading clippings with a friend is a great option to add more variety to your home environment. My favorite indoor plant is Swedish ivy. Making ivy babies is so easy! All you need to do is drop a clipping in a glass of water and nature's magic takes care of the rest. Voila!

While I do indulge in store-bought flowers, my favorite bouquets are always those that I collect myself. I have a few small flower beds to draw from, that aren't particularly productive. (I'm working on improving this with the tulip project I mentioned in chapter 1.) When it comes to flowers, I once again choose the scavenger hunt option. I'm not suggesting you trespass or do anything illegal, but our ditches and roadways are often lined with an abundance of dreamy blooms, ripe for the picking. Some of my favorite roadside finds include pussy willows, apple blossoms and lupins. In the spring I love forcing leaves and flowers, my favorite being forsythia. Cattails make interesting arrangements in the late summer and early autumn. In the winter I like to add sprigs of evergreen branches to my bouquets.

The great thing about greenery is that it doesn't add to the clutter in your home. When it has withered and run its course, it goes straight to the compost bin, ready to journey on the circle of life all over again.

Next time you are out for a Sunday drive, be sure to pack a pair of scissors!

## Catch the Sun

My favorite book from childhood is *There's a Rainbow in my Closet* by Patti Stren. I'm certain I read it a hundred times, but surprisingly I never owned a copy. I must have had it on a long-term loan from the library! Several years ago, my husband treated me to a used copy from a rare bookseller. As soon as I cracked the cover, I was transported back into Emma's world of dreaming, drawing and painting.

In the story, Emma's mother is traveling on a work commitment and her grandmother comes from afar to care for her. Struggling with her mother's extended absence, Emma initially resists developing a relationship with her grandmother. One day after school, Emma is touched and delighted to find a surprise from her grandmother—

a rainbow in her closet! Using her eyeglasses and sunlight, her grandmother creates a beautiful rainbow in an effort to connect with her troubled granddaughter.

I've admired prisms since a very young age. My own nanny had a collection hanging in her living room window, and I always delighted in studying and scrutinizing the tiny, yet vivid rainbows they produced. Inspired by this childhood story, I thought it would be fun to bring a little light, color and beauty into day-to-day family life. Although we can't control the weather, we can make an effort to infuse our lives with more rainbows!

I purchased a set of crystal prisms and hung them discretely in a few carefully selected spots in our home. Some were placed in an east-facing window to capture early morning to midday sunbeams. Another was placed in a west-facing kitchen window to catch the rays of the setting sun.

On a bright sunny morning, I enjoy admiring the colorful dancing rainbows while sipping my tea. In the afternoon, the rainbows add a touch of beauty and mystery to supper preparation. Can you imagine how dreamy these would be in a baby's room? What makes these color beams so special is that they only appear when the sun is shining brightly. They come and go as they please, elevating my mood each time they appear.

These suncatchers will work on any window that gets direct sunlight, so if you've got one, why not give it a try? You can buy these inexpensive little gems at most craft stores. (Surprise, surprise! I spotted them on Amazon.) There is no pot of gold required for rainbows of this variety, so go ahead and indulge!

## Let in the Fresh Air

Do you feel an intimate connection between your olfactory sense and your emotions? There is nothing quite like a familiar scent to send me back in time and rustle up forgotten feelings. Smells straight from nature are my favorite, of course! The sweet smell of tender spring buds, the delicious scent of lilac blooms, the salty flavour of the sea...I could create a list ten pages long of all my dreamy favorites!

Lightly draping your home with a delicate fragrance is a wonderful way to bring the outdoors in, and elevate the mood and atmosphere of a space. Of course, there are the standard options such as scented candles and essential oil diffusers. I use both of these regularly, and enjoy switching up the scents based on my mood and objectives.

My favorite method of adding a bit of flavour to my breathing space, however, is setting out a bowl of good old-fashioned potpourri! Because there are so many scented products on the market these days, I feel like this standby from the past has fallen out of favour. I prefer it because it is aesthetically pleasing to both the eye *and* the nose. Fresh flowers are beautiful, but there is something dramatically romantic about the sight of dried and wilted blooms that tugs at my heart.

It's actually pretty easy to make your own potpourri! We have an abundance of beach roses on our property (one of the few plants that thrives in these foggy parts). I collected a basket full of both petals and buds, along with some lavender from my garden. I patiently dried everything on a window screen, and after a couple of weeks, I had a generous batch of homemade potpourri to scatter around my home.

I've used the same approach in the cooler seasons when fresh flowers are not available. At Christmas I always make a set of pomanders out of clementines and cloves. I display these along with pinecones and cinnamon sticks. The spicy, woodsy scent definitely puts me in the holiday spirit.

A quick Google search for DIY recipes will get your started on your own potpourri making project. Have fun experimenting and researching your favorite scents!

I have to add just one more idea for those of you who are lucky enough to own a clothesline. You are probably already doing this, but here's a little reminder to dry your sheets on the line whenever you have the opportunity. I don't think there is *anything* that smells as delicious as line-dried sheets! You can't buy that smell in a bottle!

## Connect With the Animal Kingdom

Who doesn't love waking up to the sound of chirping birds? I love leaving my bedroom window open just a crack, (even if it's not energy efficient during the cool mornings of early spring) so I can wake up to their sweet songs.

Are you (or were you) a fan of Martha Stewart? I haven't followed her in years, but I used to watch her TV show back in the mid 2000's. As an animal lover, I always enjoyed it when she featured her pet birds on the program. Martha has been a long-time owner of canaries and finches, and she has the most lovely aviary in her home.

When my son begged me for a pet parakeet, I was pretty easily convinced, as I had memories of Martha's feathered friends in my mind. We ended up welcoming three sweet little rosy Bourke parakeets into our family. They are very low-maintenance pets. (Not all birds are! Some varieties have been compared to demanding toddlers!) They are fairly quiet, but they do make pleasant chirping sounds throughout the day, which add a solarium/sunroom vibe to our main living area. Their bird cage is not nearly as elaborate as Martha's set up, but it suits the corner of our cozy living room just perfectly.

I don't have a great track record with caring for fish, (I seem to have a deadly touch) but I absolutely love the peaceful and serene atmosphere a home aquarium provides. I find them particularly soothing to watch at night, or in the quiet darkness just before sunrise. The fluid movement of the fish, combined with the bubbling sound of the filter has such a calming effect!

I'm definitely not recommending that anyone go out and buy a pet bird or school of fish on a whim! Adopting a pet is a big decision. If, however, you have the time, budget and interest, both aquariums and aviaries add an ambiance to one's home that cannot be replicated by a nature soundtrack!

An easy and inexpensive option is to just place a bird feeder outside and allow nature to come to you. Make sure to position it within view of a window you frequent. Mine are currently on display near my kitchen window, so I can admire my feathered friends while standing at the sink. (They used to be located off the deck, but I had to move them because my dogs were going crazy all day barking at the uninvited squirrels. This was not an elevating situation!)

# ELEVATING ACTIONS AND INSPIRATION

- Making use of natural materials in your home décor allows you to invite the unique beauty of nature into your inside living spaces.

- Whenever possible, seek out the most natural and authentic materials available. Choose products and objects made of wood, stone, leather, linen, wool, cashmere, clay and beeswax. You will add a warmth and charm to your home that cannot be created in a factory or lab.

- Next time you go on a nature walk, view it as a treasure hunt. Keep on the lookout for small gifts from Mother Nature that you could bring home to decorate your house. Driftwood, pinecones, sea-shells, bird nests, unique stones, gnarly branches... all these treasures make interesting display and conversation pieces.

- Plants and greenery add warmth and light to living spaces. Have fun finding creative ways to include more live plants and flowers into your home. Pro-pagating plants is an easy and fun way to increase your inventory. For more variety in your collection, trade clippings with friends.

- Scavenge for wildflowers in your yard, the ditch or an abandoned field. (Please be aware that most public parks do not permit the removal of flora or fauna.)

Bouquets made with wildflowers have such a free and authentic feel to them.

- Keep a set of sharp scissors or small pruning shears in your car so you are always prepared to treat yourself to a roadside arrangement.

- If you have the garden space, plant your own clipping garden. Perennials and bulbs are great options as once planted, the magic of nature takes care of the rest for years to come.

- Look for fun and inspiring ways to bring the beauty of sunlight into your home. Suncatchers and prisms are inexpensive and readily available. Who wouldn't feel elevated by the sight of tiny brilliant rainbows dancing around their home?

- Heavenly aromas can help create an inviting atmosphere in your home. Scented candles, fresh flowers, and essential oil diffusers are all lovely ways to infuse a gentle scent into your rooms. Potpourri is another great natural option that you can have fun with. Experiment and try out some new recipes.

- Aviaries and aquariums add a relaxing, soothing ambiance to rooms. If it's something you are interested in, go for it. If not, put up a birdfeeder outside your favorite window and enjoy the view.

# 7

# EXERCISE YOUR FLEXIBILITY

The COVID-19 pandemic taught us all many lessons. It forced me to exercise more patience. It helped me learn to let go of what I can't control. It taught me to prioritize my commitments. It highlighted how much I love my family. It *also taught me* how much I *need a break* from my loved ones from time to time!

Did you go through a period of extended pandemic lockdown with the members of your household? While I certainly cherished and enjoyed this unexpected "quality time" together, there were moments I felt like I couldn't find five minutes of solitude. We live in a three bedroom home, and I still felt like we were crawling over each other at times!

I recognize how fortunate our family was to be living in a spacious home during the lockdown. That being said, the pandemic allowed me to step back and view our living space with fresh eyes and a new perspective. Because we were all suddenly operating under one roof, twenty-four hours a day, there were some adjustments that needed to be made to help the business of life flow more efficiently and pleasantly!

One of my favorite books on the subject of home design is, *Not So Big House: A Blueprint for the Way We Really Live* by Sarah Susanka. The author makes the point that the "Not So Big House" actually feels more spacious than its larger counterparts, because the space is designed and used with intention and purpose. The idea is that each area of your home is a "space of substance", which is used and loved every day.

While this book really focuses on new home design, I like the idea of drawing on the spirit behind the "Not So Big House" in an effort to make the best use of all rooms and areas of my home. Whether you live in a bachelor apartment or a sprawling mansion, maximizing your space for optimal productivity and enjoyment feels refreshing and uplifting.

## Put on Your Rose Colored Glasses

My husband is an avid surfer, which is one of the reasons we live by the ocean. Most people aren't aware that Nova Scotia can be the home to world class waves! During a big hurricane swell, it's not uncommon for wave chasers to travel from afar to take advantage of this obscure destination on the surfing circuit. The crowds can be quite small compared to well-known spots, so it's a great opportunity to get one's fair share of the action.

As soon as there is a whiff of hurricane action travelling up the Eastern Seaboard, my husband's phone starts lighting up. Surfers are a blood thirsty breed (or rather wave thirsty)!

Several years ago, my husband informed me that a friend from California wanted to make a last-minute trip to Nova Scotia in anticipation of the arrival of Hurricane Bill. He was planning on arriving that very night, and wanted to crash at our house. Oh, and by the way, a few of his friends would be tagging along. This was followed by, "Please don't freak out, but one of them is Brody Jenner."

I don't know if you are up on pop culture, but I clearly wasn't at the time. My reaction to this statement was, "Who the hell is Brody Jenner?" If you are as ignorant as I was, he is the son of Kaitlyn Jenner and the half-brother of Kendall and Kylie Jenner. I had heard of Kaitlyn Jenner, so I finally figured out he had some ties to the Kardashian family.

I set our guests up in the loft above our garage in full "glamping" style. One took the couch, one got a single mattress on the floor, and one was forced to contort his body to fit into an antique Acadian bed (which barely fits my 5'3" frame).

I'm sure they weren't expecting luxury accommodations, despite their "star" status, and were likely just thankful for a place to stay with easy access to the beach. They were, however, very impressed with one special area of our home!

After their first surf session, they made their way down to our unfinished basement to rinse off and warm up in the "surf shower room". This is the one room in our house that I dare not enter. We've lived here for seventeen years. I believe my husband has cleaned it once. Regardless, our guests walked into the concrete space and immediately reacted with a range of comments including words such as "cool", "whoa", "wicked", "awesome". Apparently in Malibu, there aren't many homes with unfinished basements, so our rough and ready space was viewed as edgy and innovative. Who knew we could top California cool?

As I mentioned in chapter 4, last summer I was having trouble concentrating on my writing at home. I desperately needed to get the kids out from under my feet. We needed a place to set up another TV, and the basement was the obvious choice. I felt guilty relegating them to the dungeon, but I didn't want to spend money renovating this dingy space. Memories of our surfer guests allowed me to view the basement from a different perspective. If it was good enough for these so-called celebrities, clearly my teenage boys wouldn't see any harm in moving their video game console out of my writing loft and into the hipster haven. My rose-colored glasses allowed me to view the space as the dreamy man cave that it was. My kids' reaction? "Finally we can get away from Mom!"

Have you tried looking at your own home with a pair of rose-colored glasses? There might be spaces that feel ugly and unattractive at first glance, that actually offer a brilliant solution to a perplexing problem. If you read *Love Warrior* by Glennon Doyle, you'll know she actually turned her closet into her writing room!

If you are pinched for space, creative thinking can come in handy! Put pen to paper and write down all the missing "rooms" in your current home. If your kids only use their bedrooms for sleeping, could they serve as home offices during the day? Could a walk-in closet become a quaint nursery in a pinch? Just Google "flex spaces" and you will be overloaded with inspiration and ideas.

## Let Go of Perfectionism

You don't need to fork out a ton of money to make your home functional, inviting and pretty. As families grow and interests change, our living spaces evolve along with us. Everything doesn't have to be set up perfectly for this moment in time, because this moment is fleeting! At times, it's more than acceptable to throw together a temporary set up that is "good enough" to serve your current needs.

The teen "man cave" in our basement is the perfect example. Sure, it would be nice to have a finished basement with proper drywall and flooring, but it's just not in our budget at the moment. Our jury-rigged solution isn't exactly pretty, but the kids don't seem to mind (again, I think they think it's edgy and cool). We bought a hideous black vinyl sofa off our local classifieds for $200. I despise it, but it's got that highly sought-after man cave vibe. We purchased a carpet end at the discount flooring shop for $60 to add some warmth to the space. Our biggest expense was the television, which we kept at a reasonable fifty-five inches. Again, not pretty, not perfect, but a perfectly acceptable solution.

The interesting thing to note is that the basement is still an evolving space. Who knows what the future holds? I'm not yet ready to commit to anything permanent. It has served many purposes: home gym, rug hooking studio, mini bike track, fingerboard factory, science lab, skate ramp, basketball court, splatter art studio, YouTube film studio....etc.

Do you have a need for double (or triple) duty spaces in your home? Sometimes it's not ideal, but we just have to find a way to make it work. Let go of your perfectionism and accept that your set up might not be as ideal as you would like it to be. View it as a challenge to find a way to "make do".

Like many, my husband has been working from home more than ever these days. He was forced to set up shop in our bedroom. This pretty much contradicts all my beliefs about the peaceful refuge I believe a bedroom should be. That being said, it was the best solution available. He has a booming voice, which needed to be contained. The dining room table wasn't going to cut it during his marathon conference calls. He can close the bedroom door to limit interruptions and distractions. It's also the only room in the house with an air conditioner. If he's going to spend eight to ten hours in a room, it might as well be comfortable.

My husband's home office won't likely stay like this forever, but for now, it's good enough!

## Create Your Great Escape

I live in a very masculine household, and there are times I feel the need to escape into a world of frivolity and femininity. I enjoy playing around in my closet, writing in pretty journals, reading inspiring books and adding touches of beauty to my surroundings.

In my dream world, I would have a "she-shed". If you aren't familiar with the term, this really takes the man cave to the next level!

A she-shed is an outdoor structure that serves as a dreamy, feminine getaway. Most often it is just an old garden or storage shed that has been converted into a peaceful, tranquil refuge, where a woman can indulge in her femininity and escape the demands of life! It's a place to read, dream, create and make as pretty as your little girly heart desires.

As I look out my window, I spot the wood shed and the wheels of my mind start turning. My husband dreams of converting it into a sauna, but I can't get past the fact that it served as a chicken coop for seven years. Let's just say the prior occupants left their mark. I decide to leave that project for him and focus on creating a great escape in a corner of our home.

The most peaceful room is my house is my bedroom. When it's not serving as tax accountant headquarters, it's actually one of my favorite places to spend time. It's painted in a soothing grey-blue and definitely has that breezy, coastal cottage vibe I'm always aiming to achieve. It houses so many of my favorite things such as my wardrobe, my perfumes and cosmetics, and a stack of inspiring journals and books. It's the perfect getaway!

Do you have a spot in your home that could serve as a feminine retreat? Your bedroom really is a great place to start. What inexpensive but small touches could you add to make it feel just a bit more special, soothing and serene? Here's a list to get you started:

- Fresh flowers! We often reserve them for the dining room table, but they add a sense of luxury to one's bedroom.

- A lock on the door. This might go without saying, but it's an important one!

- Relaxing scents. My go-to is always lavender as it apparently promotes relaxation.

- Yummy reading material. Who says you always have to expand your mind and read thought-provoking books. If that's what you're in the mood for, go for it, but don't feel guilty adding a bit of scandalous "chick lit" to your bedside stack. There is no shame in fantasy!

- Luxurious sheets. Buy the best ones you can afford and enjoy every moment you get to spend between them.

- A fresh coat of paint. The right color can be very effective at creating a tranquil ambiance. Most of my home is painted off-white, but I wanted my bedroom to feel special and different. If you're interested, I used *Beacon Gray* by Benjamin Moore.

- Your favorite things! Start your own list now…

I'd also like to point out that your "great escape" need not be feminine *or* pretty! As long as it allows you to relax and unwind, it is serving its intended purpose.

My other great escape is my home gym. My husband refers to it as my jail cell, because that's about the size of it. It is also located in the unfinished concrete basement. I might even choose this room over my bedroom if forced to make a choice! It's where I go to escape, workout, think, disconnect, practice self-love and just feel good! It's very basic, but it has everything I need to get in a good workout: a set of free weights, a bench, a pull up bar, a yoga mat and an itty bitty TV where I can stream my workout videos. (It's so small I've decided it doesn't even classify as a real television!) I guess it's not only the boys who like to tap into their extreme and edgy side now and then.

Could you carve out a corner of the basement or garage for your own personal pursuits that are a little on the messy side? Maybe that storage shed doesn't even need a renovation to give you that solitude you're looking for!

## ELEVATING ACTIONS AND INSPIRATION

- Aim to make the best use of all areas of your home. This will allow you to maximize the space you have available and increase your enjoyment of daily life.
- Try on a pair of rose-colored glasses when analyzing your living spaces. Ugly and uninviting areas are often gems in disguise. They can offer brilliant solutions to your space woes.
- If you are pinched for space, get creative and adopt a flexible mindset. Make a list of missing rooms and

corners in your home and set off to research "flex spaces". There are lots of great ideas out there. Chances are someone has already solved your specific problem.

- Allow your living spaces to shift and evolve as the seasons of life unfold. Choose flexible over permanent solutions to keep your options open.

- Free yourself from the rigidity of seeking out a picture perfect solution. Sometimes the best space solution is one that is good enough for the time being. It might not look pretty, but if it suits your needs and budget, roll with it.

- Find a corner of your home you can call your own. Everyone needs a little retreat to reconnect with themselves. Make it pretty and fill it with all your favorite things!

- Don't be shy to carve out an area for yourself that might look a little rough around the edges. If it serves the purpose of providing you with an escape, then it is doing its job.

# 8

# CLAMP DOWN ON CLUTTER WITH A GENTLE HAND

Decluttering has become a buzzword in the world of home organizing. Marie Kondo and her book, *The Life Changing Magic of Tidying Up* hit the world by storm, inspiring millions of people to rethink their relationships with their "stuff".

Clutter seems like such a first world problem, that it almost feels shameful and embarrassing to discuss it. It's interesting to observe that human stress can result from instances of both scarcity and abundance (or rather over-abundance). The excess stuff we amass throughout our lives takes a lot of work to manage, clean, repair, maintain, organize, sift through, climb over and ignore.

The topic of decluttering and minimalism has been beat to death, and yet we all keep coming back for more. A quick Google search for books on minimalism, decluttering and home organizing will produce *overabundant* results (that might leave you feeling overwhelmed!) After reading a good chunk of them, I don't strongly favour any one approach. I like to pick and choose what suits my lifestyle. I've tried many different techniques depending on the objects or area of my home I'm tackling.

I'm certainly not going to try to reinvent the wheel here, but I would like to add my two cents. The issue of clutter cannot be ignored when contemplating ways to elevate one's homelife. It's a big issue for many of us! If you are really gung ho and want to take your house by storm, I suggest diving into one of the many decluttering books on the market for detailed guidance.

As an everyday woman, I'm here to offer a dusting of inspiration, along with some valuable tips and insights I've come up with over the years. My ideas might inspire you to finally declutter your entire home from top to bottom, or simply view a few of your belongings with a fresh perspective. Regardless of what condition your home is in, daily life is in a constant state of change and motion. There are always areas to tweak and adjust, and even small steps can significantly improve the enjoyment you receive from your living spaces.

## Experiment with Capsules

Vacations definitely support the argument for adopting a capsule approach to our belongings. So many people complain about packing, but once they arrive at their destination, they feel liberated by having limited choices. I've always enjoyed holiday wardrobes because they are flexible, cohesive and well-thought out. (Plus, you usually pack your favorite things, so wearing your clothes is a joy.)

There are many areas within your home where adopting a capsule approach can bring a sense of ease and simplicity to your daily life. Your wardrobe is an obvious place to start .We already touched on this in chapter 3 by experimenting with the "pack for a month" approach. Did you give this exercise a try? If so, pull out your notes and see if anything insightful pops out at you. Did you enjoy having a smaller selection of items to choose from? Are you convinced that maintaining a smaller, capsule-style wardrobe might suit you? Can you think of areas of your home where a capsule collection would suit your lifestyle? No area is off-limits!

I use the capsule approach with my cosmetics. I'm not a makeup guru, so I feel like I don't need much to pull together a quick, fresh face in the morning. I maintain a very small selection of items and am spared the need to rummage through cluttered drawers to find the perfect shade of lip gloss or eyeliner.

Perhaps you only need a few carefully selected gardening tools, neatly stored and easily accessible in the shed. How many cooking pans does one need? I have just two! A round pizza pan and a large rectangular one for cookies.

Whether you are tackling your closet, kitchen or garage, keep in mind that *you* get to make the rules! There is no need to get rigid or extreme and actually pare things down to five, ten, or thirty three items. It doesn't have to turn into a numbers game to adopt the spirit of the capsule concept. If you want to free up some space both mentally and physically, you can create capsules without purging the leftovers. Store the excess out of sight for the time being. As the months roll along, take note as to whether you miss the off-site items. If you do, go ahead and dig them out. If you don't, perhaps it's time to send them on their way.

## Don't Go To Extremes

It's easy to get caught up in the minimalist mindset and get a little carried away. When my dad and I went on a cycling trip in Croatia, he gloated about how he managed to fit all his belongings into a single carry-on, while I had to check a larger bag. Needing both cycling gear and street clothes, I just couldn't swing a carry-on. I was impressed with his packing skills, until I realized he neglected to bring any socks, and only packed one shirt for seven days of cycling (and I had to spend each night sharing a tiny cabin with that smelly shirt drying on the air conditioner). Thank goodness they gave out free socks on the plane, or his shoes would have smelled as "pleasant" as his shirt.

There were times in my life where I took the concept of minimalism too far. In a quest to pare down our household belongings to the bare minimum, I ended up creating problems for myself. What works for one member of the family doesn't necessarily suit others in the house! While it might make perfect sense to include just *one pair* of nice gloves in *my* selection of winter accessories, this idea is just plain stupid when it comes to kids! Kids lose stuff... every single day. They also vomit on their sheets in the middle of the night. I've learned my lesson and take a much more generous approach when stocking the "stuff" of my children's lives.

It's easy to get caught up in the excitement when decluttering your home. Resist the urge to whittle things down to an extreme level. It's ok to have multiples and duplicates on hand, especially when children are involved.

## Don't Be Afraid to Hang On

A lot of advice in minimalist circles focuses on purging those items in our homes that are often left ignored. While I agree with the idea that we shouldn't clutter up our spaces with belongings we have little or no use for, there are many instances where hanging on to them makes perfect sense.

I've been a follower of the country lifestyle blogger Becky Cole for many years. (You can find her at www.beckyocole.com.) She posted a series of entries in 2015 and 2016 on the topic of wardrobe planning. At the time, I had just set off on a journey to elevate my personal style. I found her insights so helpful because her rural lifestyle mirrored my own. She coined the term, "Teeny Tiny Urban Wardrobe", and I've kept the concept in my back pocket ever since. The "Teeny Tiny Urban Wardrobe" is a collection of nice clothes that you might not wear that often, but are still necessary in your closet. Even country girls want to look smart and chic when they visit the city! It's okay to have a collection of really nice clothes that you save for special trips and occasions. You don't need to wear your cashmere car coat mucking out the barn!

The "teeny tiny" philosophy can be applied to so many of our belongings. It is a reminder that just because something doesn't receive regular use, doesn't mean it needs to be purged from your life if it still serves an important purpose (although rarely).

Let go of the guilt for hanging on to and safely stowing nice things, even if you only enjoy them on occasion. If you have the space for them, what's the big deal? You get to make the rules. There's nothing wrong with packing away your collections of expensive china and crystal, and only enjoying them during the holidays. It's perfectly fine to have that delicate white silk blouse hanging in your closet, even if you only reach for it on very special occasions.

Allow yourself the guilt-free luxury of a "teeny tiny" collection of delicate, expensive and fragile things!

## Use Your Best With Caution

Many of us are familiar with the concept of using and enjoying our nice things every day. Why not view each day as a celebration, and experience joy from our special belongings regularly? What is the point in saving them for an uncertain future date? I love this concept, *but* I also believe one needs to exercise caution with this approach! I've encountered a few "real life" experiences where I've been burned, and my beloved "nice things" ended up in the trash.

I once owned (note the use of the past tense) an adorable vintage glassware set I picked up at an antique store. It included a pitcher and six matching juice glasses. It was made in France and featured a sweet nautical design that complemented my coastal themed décor perfectly. Drinking from those glasses definitely elevated my breakfast routine. Sadly, the pitcher is all that remains of the set. One by one those glasses met the fate of the dustpan. I love my children dearly, but there's no denying they are rough on things.

We received a beautiful set of high quality, expensive flatware as wedding gifts. For years I had it tucked away, but one day decided to put these lovely utensils in regular rotation. I own a complete set of twelve forks, and every single one of them has warped and twisted tines. My son, the budding engineer, has found many innovative uses for them in his workshop! Of course, the pattern is discontinued, and replacing them would be expensive. For now, I'll continued eating my food off deformed forks.

Since these experiences, (and countless others) I now focus on using a "first person" approach to the "use your nice things" philosophy. *I* use *my* nice things. I spritz myself daily in expensive perfume, I use up my luxurious beauty products, I wear my favorite clothes, I drink tea from my beautiful handmade mugs, and I burn my decadent scented candles alone in my writing loft. (I have learned that open flames and science-minded children are a disastrous combination.)

Don't be afraid to be selfish with your nice things. Use and enjoy them, but hide and protect them when it is necessary! There is nothing wrong with locking up your "nice things" during certain seasons of life (kids at home) and releasing them later (kids leave nest).

## Apply the Sunk Cost Theory

As an accountant, I love drawing on my knowledge of financial theory and applying it to different areas of my life. Yes, it sounds a little geeky, but there is wisdom to be gained from my old textbooks. (I bet I could even write an entire book using this theme!)

The term "sunk cost" in accounting refers to money that has been spent and can't be recovered. Basing any decisions on a sunk cost is pointless. The past cannot be changed, and it doesn't affect the outcome of the future.

When you do encounter an object in your life that you no longer have a use for, view it as a sunk cost. People change, tastes change, and circumstances change. Let go of the guilt and don't overthink the past. Allowing it to collect dust in the basement isn't going to bring back those dollars spent. In fact, you might even benefit financially from purging it if you manage to sell it on the second-hand market.

## Stop the Purge/Buy Cycle

Do you ever feel uncomfortable with those awkward moments of silence in a conversation? Do you feel the same way about empty and quiet spaces in your home? Does the sight of a bare shelf make you want to fill it?

I think a lot of people get caught in an endless and pointless cycle of purge/buy/purge. Perhaps you just decluttered your wardrobe, and are feeling fantastic about the sight of your closet. For the first time in years, getting dressed is a breeze because you can actually *see* what you own! Your clothes have room to breathe! This moment of satisfaction is fleeting however, because before you know it, the clutter starts to creep back in. You give in to new temptations, that quickly start to fill those empty spaces.

Don't allow yourself to view your decluttering efforts as an excuse to go shopping. You aren't doing yourself any financial favors (or the earth for that matter) by just cycling stuff through your home.

There is actually something lovely, soothing and hopeful about the sight of an empty shelf. Instead of giving into the urge to fill a void, bask in the feeling of calm a blank space evokes.

## Designate Homes Within Your Home

If there is one philosophy that keeps my house running smoothly, it's the concept of having a place for everything. If every single one of your belongings has a designated home within your home, it's a lot easier for all members of the family to contribute to a clutter free environment.

Even as a child, I was drawn to this concept. I still have fond memories of the tack room at the horseback riding camp I attended. I liked spending time in this room because I was attracted to the order. Even though the space was dusty and musty, everything had a designated place. Each horse had a labelled hook for its bridle and a post for its saddle. The tack room was always tidy and organized, despite the fact the stable was bustling with children!

As you go about the process of tidying or decluttering a room, make an effort to designate a special home for each and every item. Be sure to communicate this information to all members of your family! Resist the urge to have more than one junk drawer. (Yes, I have a junk drawer.)

## Don't Be Shy To Borrow

Every now and then we are faced with an unexpected situation that we aren't prepared for. When my Californian surfer guests arrived at my doorstep, I quickly realized I didn't have enough spare bedding to keep them warm. Instead of rushing out to the closest homewares store, I called a generous friend. She gladly hooked me up with extra sheets and duvets to get me through their visit. When my guests left, I returned the washed linens to my friend. She was happy she could help, and I was happy to keep the unnecessary bulk from my linen closet.

Don't be shy to borrow and share belongings with your friends. This works really well for big ticket items like yard equipment. Before rushing out and buying something for a one-off event, consider borrowing (or renting) first.

## Maintain an Outbox

One of the best ways to keep clutter at bay is to implement a system to deal with it, *before* it actually becomes clutter. When you are cleaning out the coat closet at the end of the winter, why bother tucking away your son's snowsuit into a storage bin? I know it's tempting to hang on to their precious youth, but kids are growing beasts! If it's unlikely it will fit him next season, purge it now!

I maintain an "outbox" in our basement for all these types of items. As soon as a belonging is identified as purgeable, it heads straight to this box. Every few months I drop the box off at a charity shop. If there is anything particularly valuable in there, I will sell it if I think it's worth the effort. Most of my outbox these days contains outgrown children's clothing, shoes and sporting gear. I've got the rest of my house in pretty good order, but every now and then I do encounter something I decide to let go of.

Locate your outbox somewhere that's convenient to access, and not easy to forget about. (Mine is next to my workout room, so I pass by it daily.) You might even choose to place it in the trunk of your car, so you are one step closer to getting those unwanted objects out of your life.

## ELEVATING ACTIONS AND INSPIRATION

- A home free of clutter provides a soothing and calm living space which allows us to better relax, both mentally and physically.
- Even small tweaks and adjustments to your attitude about your belongings can have an elevating effect on your homelife.

- Experiment using a capsule approach with different groups of your belongings. Tuck away anything that is not in use and reassess it at a later date. Small collections allow us to better appreciate what we have on hand and reduce clutter and decision making.

- Avoid going to extremes! Life is not about suffering with the least number of items you can get by with. Find a balance between barely enough and too much.

- Don't let the minimalist movement make you feel guilty for hanging on to things you rarely use. Some things really are best saved for special occasions.

- Use and enjoy your nicest things, but proceed with caution. If you have children of any age in your home, there is a risk of destruction.

- Let go of unwanted things guilt-free by applying the sunk cost approach. Realize that the money is spent, regardless of whether you hang on to it or purge it.

- If it's possible and worth the time and effort, sell any unwanted items to help recoup your costs.

- Stop the cycle of purge/buy/purge. Don't use freed up storage space as an excuse to go shopping. Relish the sight of a clean, clear, empty space.

- Designate a home for every item you own. Be sure to communicate this information to all members of the household so keeping the house tidy becomes a shared responsibility.

- Don't rush out to the store every time an unexpected need arises. Look into clutter friendly options such as borrowing or renting.
- Keep an outbox handy to store items that you wish to purge. As soon as you identify something that should go, drop it straight into the box. Regularly deliver your donations to a charity shop before the pile gets out of control.

# 9

# TACKLE HOUSEHOLD PROBLEMS LIKE A SUPERHERO

I f my mom was the fairy in the house growing up, my dad was definitely the superhero. He is always the one to swoop in and solve a problem, no matter how big or small. He definitely follows the "good enough" philosophy I discussed in chapter 7. His solutions are rarely pretty or perfect, but they usually accomplish the goal at hand.

Long before I owned my own home, my dad demonstrated the beauty and flexibility of unfinished basement space. He built three airplanes in ours while I was growing up. (Airplane building, however, is definitely a hobby where one should be striving for perfection!) He encountered many puzzles and problems on these projects, but always managed to figure his way out of a scrape.

One particular problem-solving episode comes to mind. When his first airplane was complete, and it was time to move it out of the basement, he realized he had made an error in his calculations. The fuselage did not fit through the window as he had planned. Never one to give up, he came up with a solution that got the job done. He waited until my mom went away on a girls' trip, and then smashed a giant hole in the foundation. I remember standing on the lawn, watching as the heavy machinery crumbled the concrete. I had a sinking feeling Mom was not going to be pleased upon her return Sunday evening!

While this story certainly teaches a lesson in the value of planning ahead, it also reminds us that we can all be our own superheroes. By putting on our "thinking capes", we can solve most of life's issues, irritations and problems. It's a great way to approach dealing with annoying household issues that grate on your nerves every day. Imagine how elevated you will feel once that leaky faucet is finally fixed!

## Sweat the Small Stuff

I love sharing favorite books! One tiny one that made a big impression on me is *Don't Sweat the Small Stuff...and It's All Small Stuff: Simple Ways to Keep the Little Things from Taking Over Your Life* by Richard Carlson. It offers great advice on how to reduce stress and anxiety by keeping things in perspective.

Not sweating the small stuff is a great philosophy to live by. While I agree with it in theory, let's be honest, there are times in life when *sweating the small stuff,* and tackling an irritating issue can have a very elevating effect! Sometimes, all that is required is an itty bitty tweak to a household system.

My boys are really into mountain biking. In fact, they turned our backyard into a mountain bike park. Last spring I was feeling exasperated by the state of my floors. Although they were taking their shoes off before entering, they were tracking a ton of mud in the house off their clothes. I'm not exaggerating when I say they were coated from head to toe in the stuff. Even a trip from the door to the laundry room was a housekeeping disaster.

I finally took matters into my own hands. I placed a plastic laundry hamper inside the garage that was designated for mountain biking clothes. They were told they had to strip down to their undies *before* entering the house. The dirty laundry could then be shaken out (or hosed off) outside before bringing it into the house. It sounds like a very small adjustment, but it had a huge impact on the condition of my floors! The laundry basket by the door proved to be a much more effective solution than my nagging.

What irritates you around your home? Be honest, vent, get it out! Give yourself permission to complain, and then record all your troubles in a pretty little journal. Then sit down and put on that superhero thinking cape.

Are you tripping over shoes every time you walk in the door? How long would it take to sort through the pile? Purge those that no longer fit the kids, relegate off-season pairs to storage, and find an attractive display rack for your everyday inventory. A quick, painless effort and voila, problem solved! Honestly, the solutions to life's little nuisances often involve very little effort. I always like to borrow from Nike when it comes to this sort of thing; "Just do it!"

## Become a Handy-Woman

Our homes take a lot of abuse, as least that is my experience as a mom of boys! The second hardest hit area of my home is the wall space (the first is the area around the toilets). Over the years, our walls developed something I like to refer to as "ring around the house". Years of sticky fingers, dinky cars and rough housing had definitely left a glaring mark. Every new ding and scratch left me feeling defeated.

My husband argued there was no point in paying someone to paint our house until the boys had left the nest. I agreed, it felt like a waste of money.

When the boys finally smashed a giant hole in *my* bedroom wall, (my relaxing, peaceful haven) I realized I could no longer just stand by without taking action. I simply couldn't wake up to the sight of that gaping cavity each morning. My husband is normally the one who looks after household maintenance issues, but as a tax accountant, he was smack in the middle of busy season, and didn't have a minute to spare. A quick search on YouTube gave me all the information I needed to patch the mess up myself. I finished off my plastering with a fresh coat of paint on the assaulted wall. The sight of one clean and perfect wall left me craving more. I decided I might as well paint the whole bedroom…you might be able to guess where this lead me.

Over the period of two months, I ended up painting every room in my house! Again, YouTube guided me through the whole process as I was new to the painting profession. I learned how to properly patch, tape, cut, color match and refit damaged hot water heaters!

Although the task of painting my home felt intimidating and overwhelming at first, the experience left me feeling empowered. I no longer had to cringe at the sight of yet another nick in the drywall, because I could now easily fix these minor wounds on my own! The final results were unbelievably uplifting, and I saved thousands of dollars with the do-it-yourself approach. I'm now convinced that a coat of paint is pure magic.

Do you have simple maintenance issues around your home that need to be addressed? Do you find yourself nagging your partner every weekend to get to work on his "honey-do list"? Maybe it's time for you to become the handy-woman around the house. I'm not suggesting you need to go out and get your electrician's license, but there is something very gratifying about mastering new skills. (Might I add that the shop suit I recommended in chapter 5 would add a very elevated and official vibe to your efforts!)

## Find a Cheap Fix

As an accountant who likes to stick to her household budget, I'm always looking for a cheap fix. This is exactly why the California cool man cave felt like such a great idea!

It's not only the walls and toilets that take a beating in my home. The upholstered furniture has experienced its fair share of abuse. Our couch has been peed on more times than I care to count. Jealous of the arrival of his new baby brother, this was a favorite in my eldest's bag of tricks to get my attention. He was and is a smart boy. I came running every time! Now that the kids are grown, it's the puppy peeing on it. I can't win!

Someday, the couch will be replaced, but now is certainly not the time to do it. Instead, I opted for a cheap fix. After years of being peed on, pummelled and washed, the back cushions were misshapen and droopy. I took them to an upholsterer to see what he could do to plump them up. He charged me just $80 to restuff them. They are as good as new, and cost a lot less than my dream couch!

Pull out that list of grievances you just created. Is there anything on there that you could tackle with a cheap fix? YouTube is always a great resource for ideas. Google your problem, and as I said before, no doubt someone has already solved it.

Here's a list of a few easy skills I learned to get you started. They sound so simple, it's hard to believe I had to look up the proper way to do them! Over the years, I've gotten in the habit of relying on my husband to handle most of the little maintenance issues around the house. Now that I have this knowledge, it's incredibly satisfying to eliminate irritations all by myself.

- Properly repair a hole in the drywall
- Fix my smelly dishwasher
- Remove a toilet so I could paint behind it
- Remove sticker residue from every surface in my kids' rooms
- Jump-start my car (perhaps pathetic that I didn't know this)
- Strip and refinish furniture
- Clean the filter on my washing machine
- Start the lawnmower on my own (again, pathetic)

# Maintain a Home Journal

Save yourself future headaches by staying on top of regular home maintenance. It's important to keep track of things that are easy to lose track off!

You won't be surprised that I have found a way to incorporate the use of a pretty journal into keeping track of some of the less glamourous jobs around the home. I maintain a checklist of monthly and annual chores that need to be completed, so they don't slip my mind.

The list includes tasks such as ordering firewood, servicing the furnace, sweeping the chimneys, undercoating the vehicles and pumping the septic tank. (Our septic is pumped every three years and is definitely something one does not want to forget!)

Store your journal in a handy place so that all members of your household can take ownership for these shared responsibilities. I actually have a section called, "Hubby's To-Do's" to help highlight those things that he needs to take care off. This helps reduce nagging just a little!

# ELEVATING ACTIONS AND INSPIRATION

- Make a list of all the small, irritating maintenance issues around your home that are driving you crazy. Stop procrastinating and start problem solving! Dealing with these daily nuisances once and for all will feel freeing and fantastic.

- Don't be afraid to learn new skills so you can take matters into your own hands. I guarantee, there is a "how to" YouTube video on pretty much any topic you can dream up. Roll up your sleeves and adopt a do-it-yourself mindset. You will save money *and* feel empowered!

- There are times in life when a full out renovation or upgrade doesn't make sense. You might be facing budgetary constraints, or you might be in a season of life that puts your belongings through a lot of abuse. Making do and finding a cheap and effective fix is both satisfying and uplifting.

- Create a system to keep track of household maintenance tasks that happen infrequently, but on a regular schedule. Getting ahead of the game, and staying on top of these jobs will help save you from future headaches and emergency calls to the furnace repair man in the dead of winter! (I speak from experience.)

- Make sure everyone in the household takes owner-ship for this list so that you can all pitch in and share in the responsibility of keeping your homelife running smoothly.

# 10

# COMBAT CABIN FEVER

My father literally grew up in a log cabin in the woods, in the remote mining community of Wawa, Ontario. Back then, the only way in and out of Wawa was by railroad or float plane. (A road was finally built in 1960.) There was no running water in their home. You had your choice of the outhouse or the pee pot under the bed (which was always frozen on a winter's morning). Although their cabin was eventually wired for electricity, there was just one fuse, so running more than two lightbulbs at a time was out of the question! There was no phone and no radio reception, (due to interference from ore deposits from the mine) but certainly lots and lots of books!

To this day, I always enjoy hearing stories from my father's childhood. One of my favorites is the tale about the night the family awoke to a bear climbing through their bedroom window. My grandfather, who always kept a rifle by his bed, shot the bear without even getting out from under the covers! He then went back to sleep (and thankfully took photos the next morning to provide proof to future generations). This tale from the "Melville Family Book of Lore" certainly offers a glimpse of the rustic and isolated nature of cabin life!

Reflecting on these stories of my father's childhood, I'm pretty sure this must be where the term "cabin fever" originated!

I'm guessing cases of cabin fever soared straight across the globe during the COVID-19 lockdowns. As a home-body, I didn't mind being forced to stay home at the beginning. As time wore on, however, even this introvert felt like the walls were starting to close in a little.

I hate to complain (it *does* feel good sometimes though). I know I have it pretty good living in my spacious home. No doubt my grandmother would roll her eyes if she heard me whining about feeling cooped up in my modern home, complete with all the new age luxuries and inventions she could never dream of! (Wi-Fi, smart appliances, Netflix, Xbox…etc.) Despite this, the feelings that result from being confined too long at home are real and legitimate and should not be ignored!

I've been a stay-at-home mom for over sixteen years, so I consider myself an expert on identifying the symptoms of cabin fever! The illness tends to present differently, depending on your age or species. It's definitely contagious, and in no time can spread to all members of the family (pets included).

For kids and canines, symptoms include climbing furniture and walls and making high-pitched noises. When it comes to adults, the first signs might be a little harder to detect, although I can usually tell when I'm slipping into a shack-wacky state. I start to feel listless, bored, and restless. My state of irritability skyrockets and is usually exacerbated by the previously mentioned high pitched noises!

Lockdown or no lockdown, cabin fever can strike at any time. It's important to find ways to hit the reset button and snap ourselves out of this state. Often it doesn't take more than a change of scenery or mindset to get you headed down the path of recovery.

## Rain, Shine or Snow—Get Outside

The most effective cure for cabin fever is to physically leave the cabin! Although this common sense solution is glaringly obvious, it can often be a challenge to push ourselves out the door.

I'll be the first to admit that the weather can be a drag. As a Canadian, winter is definitely the most trying time of year for me. I'm convinced I'm genetically programmed to fully hibernate like a lot of other mammals.

I'm one of those people who is *always* cold, even with the woodstove cranked. During the coldest months of the year, I really have to push myself to get outdoors. I've made a pact with myself that no matter the weather, I have to at least spend a bit of time outside each day.

I realize this message is on repeat, (I've mentioned it in my previous three books) but properly outfitting yourself for the weather has a huge impact on your ability to actually *enjoy* being outside! During the winter, I live by the motto "dress for the weather", and while you're at it, do so in style!

Although I love the breezy easiness of summer clothing, I feel more authentically myself when I'm suited up in cozy sweaters, jeans and leather boots. Topping off my ensemble with a fabulous (and warm) coat is really the icing on the cake for me.

I own a collection of winterwear that I absolutely adore. I have a fitted urban-chic down parka for really cold days. My wardrobe also contains a number of lighter wool coats, including a classic navy peacoat from J. Crew that I've had for years. This summer I snagged an outstanding deal on a tweed jacket by one of my favorite Canadian brands, Smythe. I've had this on my wish list for over five years, and it finally popped up on the preloved market for just over $100. Somehow, looking forward to wearing all these beloved pieces helps take the bite out of winter! Dare I say I'm even looking forward to it?

Depending on where you live, it might actually be the heat keeping you cooped up. I realize that scorching temperatures are a reality in many parts of the world (and sadly it seems to be getting worse). If this is your reality, you no doubt have your own techniques for beating the heat and finding ways to sneak time outside. When we do experience a heat wave in these parts, the best I can do is wake as early as possible to enjoy the great outdoors before the sun rises.

## De-Witch the Witching Hour

If you have or had little ones in your life, you are probably very well acquainted with the concept of the "witching hour". I'm referring to the time of day, usually late afternoon, when your child turns into a little devil or goblin! The symptoms greatly resemble those of cabin fever.

With both my kids in their teens, I assumed the days of the witching hour were behind me; until I got my dogs. It turns out that they too transform into little monsters as the afternoon winds down.

If you've read a lot of motivational self-help books, you are probably very familiar with recommendations around the importance of establishing morning and evening routines. These routines serve as the bookends to our days, and allow us to begin and end each one on a positive note.

While I've always embraced both morning and evening routines into my schedule, several months ago I noticed there was something missing. With so much focus on how to start and finish our days, where was the advice on how to make it *through* the days? More specifically, how does one survive the witching hour, or rather *de-witch* it? When late afternoon hits and your energy slumps at work, or the kids (or dogs) start going crazy, or you find yourself scarfing down an entire box of crackers…what can you do to reboot your hard drive to avoid total meltdown?

Enter the *afternoon routine.* The afternoon routine is so important because it serves to elevate the time of day most of us are at our worst. It's actually a concept I came upon accidentally. I noticed myself experiencing worse afternoon slumps, which seemed to coincide with the exact time of day that my sweet little poodle Coco turned into a miniature werewolf.

In an effort to elevate my afternoon, I decided to shake things up. I tried doing one of my *favorite activities* during my *least favorite* time of the day. I added a short fifteen-minute walk with Coco, smack in the middle of the afternoon slump/witching hour.

I was so happy with the elevating effect it had on both of us, that I've continued the tradition of quick afternoon escapes ever since (rain, shine or snow!) My dogs are able to release pent up energy, and I enjoy just being outdoors.

I always come home feeling refreshed, ready to tackle my upcoming obligations of preparing supper, chauffeuring children and helping with homework.

Do you find yourself or those around you in desperate need of some de-witching? Pull out your journal and start thinking of some short actions you could incorporate into your afternoons. Maybe you are looking to just relax for a few minutes, or perhaps you are in need of an energy boost. Here are a few ideas to get you started on mapping out an afternoon routine that is tailor made just for you!

- Take a walk outside, even if you only have time for a few minutes.
- If you can swing it, have short nap. Set an alarm so you don't doze for more than roughly twenty minutes. Anything beyond that and your body might want to settle in for the night!
- Have a healthy snack to get you through until dinner time. Plan ahead for this snack so it doesn't end up being a box of crackers (I speak from experience!)
- Sit down for ten minutes with a cup of tea or coffee. If you can't handle caffeine late in the day, choose a decaffeinated option. I usually pair my tea with a special chocolate peanut butter ball (the ones hidden in my freezer). It's definitely something I look forward to!
- If your small children are allotted a certain amount of screen time each day, now is the time to cash in on it!

When my kids were little, I always gave them their hour of cartoons in the late afternoon. I'd either take a nap or get a start on supper.

A rejuvenating afternoon routine is something to look forward to each day. While I'm looking at it from a homelife perspective, a lot of these ideas can also be applied if you work outside the home (or when you get home from work).

## Create Household Escapes

There are times when escaping within your home is the best option available. I mentioned in chapter 7 that my bedroom is one of my favorite rooms in our house. I have it set up to feel like a relaxing little escape where I can indulge in reading or playing around with my favorite things.

The bathroom also serves as a perfect retreat within your home. On a stormy Sunday afternoon, treat yourself to an at-home spa day. I love the atmosphere at the spa, as well as all the special little touches they add to elevate the entire experience. Any time I visit the spa, I try to take note of everything from the scented candle burning on the table, to the background music, to the techniques used by the estheticians.

Last time I was in for a facial, my esthetician wrapped my feet in warm towels while my mask was setting. It felt heavenly! I promised myself in that moment to incorporate this simple effort into my home beauty routine. She actually gave me a great tip to try that I just have to share! Heat your towels in your crock pot for an authentic spa experience!

Creating an attractive outdoor space around your home is a technique that allows you to escape the confines of your walls, without having to travel very far. This minor change in scenery can provide a much needed break from not only the monotony of your indoor surroundings, but the other occupants of the house as well.

Even a small deck can feel like a little oasis if you set it up attractively. A few potted plants, a set of wind chimes, and an inviting lounge chair can turn your tiny area into a restorative getaway. Yes, you can even sit on your deck in the winter! Bundle up, grab a warm drink, pop up a birdfeeder and sit back and enjoy the company!

## Ignite Your Own Enthusiasm

In my experience, there is nothing that cures a case of cabin fever better than an electrifying boost of your own enthusiasm.

I wrote my first book, *Elevate the Everyday* during round one of the pandemic lockdowns. Round three of lockdowns in my area resulted in the release of my third title, *Elevate Your Health*.

There comes a point where you need to reach within and ignite your own fire inside. If you've got excess energy bubbling inside you, why not spend it doing something creative and/or productive?

I got myself so revved up about the possibility of self-publishing a book, I quickly became immersed in my writing. I felt like I was running on high octane fuel, instead of enduring the woes of a worldwide lockdown.

On those days you find yourself stuck inside, view it as an opportunity. How could you inspire yourself into action? What can you get excited about? Do you want to get in the best shape of your life? Start an at-home workout routine today. Do you want to tackle a home improvement project? Draft up a budget and get some ideas down on paper today. Identify a goal or dream and jump at the chance to get the ball rolling on it.

## ELEVATING ACTIONS AND INSPIRATION

- We all catch a case of cabin fever now and then. It's important to identify when you are slipping into this state. Create a list of tricks to pull out when you need to elevate your mood and mindset.

- Make a point of getting outside every day, no matter the weather. Escaping your home, even if it's just for a short period of time, allows you to clear your head. You will appreciate your living space more upon your return.

- Work around the weather challenges you face. If it's cold, bundle up in a fabulous coat and scarf. If it's raining, grab a colorful umbrella and a cheerful raincoat.

- If hot temperatures are creating issues for you, look for ways to beat the heat. Rise before the sun to get your taste of the outdoors. If it's available, take advantage of any opportunity to cool off and get wet.

- Map out an afternoon routine that you can look forward to each day. This will help you, and others around you, get through the afternoon slump.

- Create your own escape at home. Lock the bathroom door and pamper yourself with an at-home spa treatment.

- Create a small outdoor space on your deck or door step that serves as a teeny tiny retreat. Make it pretty with plants, flowers, furniture, windchimes, or even a small fountain!

- Ignite yourself with some enthusiasm. Start a new project you've been dreaming of. It's amazing how much energy can be produced from within when you are living in an inspired state.

# 11

# LOVE YOUR PERFECTLY IMPERFECT HOME

As a child of the eighties, I was a huge fan of the movie *Annie*. I spent hours in my basement, (unfinished, of course!) re-enacting its scenes and singing along loudly to the soundtrack. My favorite musical/dance performance from the movie was *It's the Hard Knock Life*. It wasn't just the catchy tune that captured my heart, but also the manner in which the actors made household chores look fun (even while wearing rags and living in a dingy orphanage). Let's be honest, backflips, cartwheels and choreographed dance routines would elevate pretty much any task!

I used to play this particular song on repeat while doing *my own* chores, which I actually *enjoyed*! Cleaning the bathroom was at the top of my list. Even back then, there was something incredibly satisfying about the sight of a sparking sink.

My, things have changed! While I still swoon at the sight of glistening porcelain, cleaning doesn't seem to spark the same degree of enthusiasm and imagination as it did back then. It's not that I dislike cleaning. I still find it incredibly rewarding to transform a space from disordered to ordered; from grungy to pristine. I think it comes down to the fact that I'm no longer living in the fantasy-land of childhood! As an adult, I'm juggling all the responsibilities of running a busy household. Maintaining a clean and tidy home is just *one* task on the endless to-do list of life!

In each one of my books, I like to include a letter to myself. The purpose of *this* chapter is to not only inspire my readers, but also myself! Maybe it's time for all of us to ask ourselves these questions. When did the household chores start to feel like such a drag? Why is it so hard to keep the house in tip top shape? When did my home start to feel like a heavy burden on my shoulders? How could we do things differently? Better yet, how could we *view* things differently?

## Appreciate The Comforts of Home

During the summer of 1996, my father and I cycled across Canada. After graduating from university, I wanted to embark on a celebratory adventure before settling into my full-time job at an accounting firm. Travelling by pedal power forces one to live a bare bones lifestyle! We slept in a tent most nights, so we were forced to live without the many comforts of home. Interestingly, tent life taught me that I didn't need much at the end of the day to feel comfortable and content. A warm meal, a hot shower at the campground, and a dry sleeping bag all felt luxuriously satisfying after a long day on the road.

This is the same sentiment my father expressed when I asked him about his experience growing up in that remote log cabin, "Did I grow up poor? Sure didn't! I had everything I wanted and was spoiled rotten; a slingshot, a fishing rod, a bow and arrow set, Lone Ranger cap guns and snowshoes. I was the "King of the World" long before Mohammed Ali."

I love his words, because they are a charming reminder of just how rich our lives can be, regardless of the home we live in, or the belongings we fill it with.

I tend to believe that the hashtags *#blessed* and *#grateful* have been so overused, that we may have become numb to their meaning. That being said, I think it's worthwhile to pause in this moment and make a small list of the sweet pleasures in your life at home. At the end of a long day, what do you love coming home to? I'm guessing your list might not include the overpriced granite countertops, or the designer handbag collecting dust in your closet. It's the simple things that hit a home run: your ecstatic dog greeting you at the door, sinking under the soft covers at night, tucking in your kids with a bedtime story, sitting in a state of quiet on the couch, savoring a warm home-cooked meal, sliding into a soothing bath...etc. It's always helpful to take note of just how little we need to feel content! Pull out your list any time you need a gentle reminder of the riches in your life.

## Avoid Temptation

Just as having a giant stash of chips in the house is going to stir your cravings, so does immersing yourself in fashionably styled images of perfect homes! Despite my interest in house design and décor, I keep my distance from home decorating magazines. I also don't follow social media influencers who tend to post *picture perfect* images of *picture perfect* home life. (Remember from chapter 3, I am now wise to the world, and realize such perfection does not exist!)

While I too try to post inspiring images on my Instagram account, (believe me it's a struggle) I don't try to stage something that is unrealistic. I find that many glossy magazine pages and filtered social media posts have such an unattainable look to them, that they leave me feeling cold. Instead of being inspired, I sometimes feel envious, ungrateful and unhappy with my own good fortune. The more I browse picture perfect images, the more I want to renovate, redecorate and redo. It's not a head space I enjoy spending time in. The truth is, I feel more elevated that I'm directing funds to my retirement savings than a new kitchen counter. My Instagram feed, however, isn't exactly overflowing with pretty images of quiet bank transfers to a savings account!

My advice is, if something makes you feel bad, stay away from it. Shift your focus to *your real life,* (as opposed to these staged lives). Seek out small steps or changes that will serve to elevate your mood, mindset and the experience of *real life* at home!

## Set Priorities

Are you also feeling rundown and overwhelmed by the sheer volume of household tasks and chores? The reality is, life is messy. It takes a lot of work to maintain spotless living spaces. I live with five males (one husband, two teen boys, two male dogs). Since I'm working on complaining less, I'll just leave it at that and allow you to read between the lines!

Although the fairyland version of my home would be immaculately clean and organized at all times, I'm just not willing do to what it takes to achieve this level of perfection. There are so many other obligations and interests that are beckoning my attention. It's especially easy to fall into the trap of constantly cleaning if you spend most of your days at home. There comes a point when you need to set some boundaries and priorities when it comes to housework. Only you will know how to find that sweet spot. Is it time to drop the mop and read a book to your child? Is it time to let the clothes sit in the dryer while you sneak away for half an hour to work on your novel?

My approach has been to relax my standards, while still keeping the house in an acceptable state. I focus on key areas, and lower my standards in the secondary spaces.

The kitchen is the big one. Keeping this area in decent order takes a team effort in my house, and both my husband and I put a lot of work into maintaining an acceptable level of cleanliness in this room. I also focus on the areas of the home that are mine, and mine alone. These include my bathroom vanity, my closet, my workout room and my home office space. Having these personal spaces in perfect condition fills my instinctual need for order! It allows me to turn a blind eye to the rest of the home (and in particular, any area my son the scientist/engineer conducts his research and experiments!)

Is it time to lower *your* standards? This is easier to do if you set aside those special corners of your home as priorities. Make a list of certain areas of your home where cleanliness and order are a top priority. Commit to focusing your efforts on these designated areas, while lowering your expectations on other spots in your home. The kitchen is an obvious choice, but try to include those spaces that are special to you! Think back to chapter 7.

Did you identify an area of your home that serves as a "great escape"? Maybe you will choose to make your bedroom a priority, so that you have a place of calm to retreat to when the rest of the house is in disarray. You might commit to making your bed each morning, ensuring your dresser and bedside table are neat and tidy, and that all clothes are properly put away instead of slung over a chair.

## Have a System

I've never been one of those people who could stick to a cleaning schedule or routine. While I love the old-fashioned notion of having a day of the week set aside for certain tasks, this approach simply never suited my lifestyle. With all of us going in different directions, one week never resembles another! I'm constantly adjusting and re-adjusting our schedules to make sure everyone gets to where they need to be, and the necessities get accomplished.

If you do run your household on a strict schedule, I applaud you! I think the key is finding a system that work for *you* and that allows you to accomplish your goals around the house (while maintaining flexible standards of course!)

No matter what your situation is, I think it's worthwhile to put a little thought into the systems and processes you have in place for getting things done. There are lots of great books on the topic of household management. If you are interested in diving deeply into this area, I recommend

*Sink Reflections* by Marla Cilley, aka "The FlyLady". Her approach is quite thorough and structured, but I enjoyed picking and choosing helpful tidbits to incorporate into my own life.

Because I am home most days, I tend to pick away at things throughout the day. If I'm feeling particularly energetic, I might take on a large task. Other times I squeeze in a toilet scrub or sink wipe down in passing. Over the years, I've put a few tricks in place to keep things running as smoothly as possible around my home. Use my ideas as a starting point and create your own philosophy or approach to housekeeping. It's fun to look at things from a fresh perspective and shake things up now and then. Investing some thought into the more mundane tasks in life can help achieve this.

- My daily to-do list includes cleaning. I may decide to tackle something big like defrosting the freezer, or I may simply make note to do a five minute quick tidy in the living room. **Writing it down** allows for the satisfaction of crossing it off!

- I adopted a policy to "**never leave a room empty handed**". In a busy household, objects often stray from their homes. I'm constantly returning them to their designated spots (as discussed in chapter 8) as I go about my business. It's an easy and effective way to stay on top of clutter. Since you already know where each item belongs, it requires very little mental energy! If someone else is headed upstairs, they are usually handed an item to deliver to its home on their way by.

- I **set a timer** if I don't want to get lost in a task. (This is recommended by The FlyLady.) If I'm working on a new book and want to make sure I make time to write, I don't allow myself to drown in my own perfectionist tendencies. If the room isn't as clean as I'd like it to be, I can always come back to it later...or learn to live with its imperfect state.

- I use **yummy smelling cleaning products**! The experience of cleaning the bathroom is definitely elevated by the soothing scent of lavender. There are lots of recipes online for do-it-yourself natural cleaners. I just use the store-bought versions and am happy with their performance and uplifting nature.

- I **reward myself regularly** for my efforts. Although the sight of a sparkling clean room is often reward enough, I do like to dangle small treats in front of my nose to push myself to do things I'm not particularly excited about. That quiet cup of tea pared with guilt-free Instagram scrolling can appear very appealing when faced with a mountain of laundry to fold!

- Keeping the house in order is not your sole responsibility. Obviously, **all members of the household should be pitching in on keeping things running smoothly.** I'd love to report that I am a master at delegation, but the truth is I'm not. My husband helps out where he can, but he also works very long hours at the office. My kids do a few household tasks, but could definitely be pitching in more. It's hard to strike a balance as it really comes down to their individual needs and priorities. If they are spending a lot of time on homework, then their plates have a very small side-serving of chores. It's a constantly evolving situation that I revisit often.

- I have also **enlisted outside help** during different seasons of my life. When I went back to work very pregnant with my second child, I hired cleaners to come in every two weeks. Other times, I've hired them to help with seasonal tasks such as window cleaning. Recently, since I started writing, I've had them tend to certain areas that are always left ignored (base-boards). I decided it was worth allocating a small portion of this new income source towards a cleaning service, as it allows me to spend more time creating my books. This could change in the future, but it suits my situation for now. The key thing to keep in mind is that there is **no shame in seeking out help** (or admitting that you use it).

## ELEVATING ACTIONS AND INSPIRATION

- When feeling weighed down by the heavy burden of household responsibilities, a shift in your attitude and mindset can serve to lighten the load.

- Take a few moments to record a list of the most delicious comforts of home. Allow the feeling of appreciation to soak in as you reflect on these simple, yet pleasurable riches in your life.

- Avoid surrounding yourself with images that leave you feeling disappointed, envious, unsatisfied and yearning for more.

- Spend your time focusing on *your* real life, home and relationships, instead of the staged ones offered on social media.

- Designate certain areas of your home as top priority and feel free to let the other secondary zones slide. Choose to focus on those rooms or spaces that will have a high impact on your mood.

- It's worth it to sit back and analyze how you go about accomplishing the more mundane tasks in life. Sometimes a new approach or perspective can add a touch of enthusiasm to something you normally dread doing.

- If you are looking to completely revamp your housekeeping systems, read a book on the topic for detailed advice and inspiration.

- Adopt little habits to increase productivity and enjoyment around your home. Make lists, use a timer, indulge in pleasant cleaning products, offer small self-rewards and don't be shy to seek help when you need it.

# 12

# 100 SEASONAL IDEAS TO ELEVATE LIFE AT HOME

As humans and creatures of this earth, the seasons play an important role in our lives. They affect our activities, the foods we eat, the clothes we wear, and certainly, how we spend our days at home.

I've always felt that being in touch with nature and the shifting seasons allows me to feel more grounded in the present moment. Living a life that celebrates each unique season feels richer and more gratifying.

I thought it would be fun to cap off this book with a list of inspiring ideas to welcome the magic that each season has to offer into our lives at home. It serves as an exercise to get your own creative juices flowing. I've started you off with twenty-five ideas per season, but don't stop there! Grab your journal and start dreaming.

# Winter

1. Welcome the quiet and cold starkness of winter. View it as a time to cozy up your home.

2. Enhance the cozy vibe of your home with woodsy scents such as pine and fir. Scented candles add the bonus of a little extra light during this dark time of year.

3. This is the perfect time to defrost your freezer. You can store your frozen foods on the porch while you are tackling the task.

4. Shovel your walkway with gratitude. Be thankful for the opportunity to get exercise while enjoying the crisp winter air.

5. Create a display of dried goods in your pantry. Store your lentils, beans, pasta and rice in large glass jars. They will inspire you to cook comfort food that is both satisfying and healthy.

6. Even though it's winter, there are still hidden treasures to hunt and scavenge for on nature walks. Sprigs of evergreens, bare branches and pinecones all add interesting and natural touches to your home décor.

7. If you feel yourself getting a little shack wacky, bundle up and get outside. You will appreciate your home even more when you come in from the frigid outdoors.

8. If you can swing it in your budget, book yourself a massage or spa treatment. Escaping to a state of bliss is a great cure for cabin fever.

9. Treat yourself to a spa day at home. Wrap yourself in a luxurious robe and pamper yourself with a face mask, body scrub and pedicure.

10. Set yourself up with a collection of cozy and attractive winter loungewear.

11. Buy or borrow a book on the topic of hygge, the Danish concept of cozy contentment.

12. It's the perfect season to force amaryllis and narcissus bulbs indoors. Enjoy the treat of these gorgeous blooms in the dead of winter.

13. Set up a space or corner in your home for fitness activities. Don't let the cold weather be your excuse to become a couch potato.

14. Add an extra dose of coziness to your bed. Layer up with a puffy duvet or an extra soft fleece blanket.

15. Focus on indoor home improvement projects. You might as well take advantage of being indoors by finally accomplishing long standing items on your to-do list.

16. Organize your photographs once and for all. This is a great way to pass a lazy Sunday afternoon. You will feel uplifted reminiscing about fond memories *and* getting them organized.

17. Indulge in some bubble gum chick lit. Everyone deserves a winter escape to fantasy land.

18. Pretend you are on a mountain holiday and set yourself up for an evening of après-ski activities at home. Put your feet up by the fire, indulge in a cheese fondue and pull out the boardgames.

19. Tuck sachets of dried flowers and potpourri in your lingerie drawer. On a gloomy winter day, enjoy the sweet scent of summer next to your skin.

20. Winter is a season we naturally crave rest. Nap unapologetically when you want to!

21. Invest in the comfiest, coziest pair of slippers you can find to keep yourself warm from the bottom up.

22. Look for ways to heat things up inside. I love cuddling up with a microwaveable heating pad on my lap.

23. Pass the evenings with a new or old hobby. Knitting on a cold winter's night feels cozy. As a bonus, you can make pretty winter accessories such as scarves and hats.

24. Look for ways to add more light to your life. If you are susceptible to the blues during the season of darkness, consider investing in a mood-boosting light therapy device.

25. Fill your home with as much greenery as possible. Adding plants to a room brings warmth and life to a space.

# Spring

1. Even if there is still a chill in the air, open up your bedroom window a crack. Spring is the best season to wake early to the beautiful sounds of songbirds!
2. Embrace this season of fresh starts. Look around your home and identify anything that is grungy and in need of replacement. Spring is a fun time to replace old dishcloths with something clean and pretty.
3. Pick a small dingy space in your home and give it a fresh coat of paint. After a messy winter, the front entry-way is a great place to start. It's amazing what a fresh coat of paint can do to elevate a space.
4. Take advantage of the early sunrises. This is the perfect season to slow down your mornings by getting up a bit earlier. Savour the extra time to relax and enjoy your home before the busy day begins.
5. Give Mother Nature a shove. Cut a collection of branches and force the blooms indoors. Forsythia, magnolia and apple blossoms are great ones to try.
6. Buy those delicate fresh tulips! They might not last long, but their short-lived beauty is worth the cost.
7. Embrace natural spring scents into your home. Hyacinths have such a strong and lovely fragrance. When you see those little potted bulbs on sale at the

grocery store, go ahead and treat yourself to this inexpensive pleasure.

8. Even though winter is over, it doesn't mean you have to put away the bird feeder. Spring is a great time to spot migratory birds. Buy yourself a bird book so you can identify your visitors.

9. Allow yourself to catch spring fever. Let your enthusiasm take over and tackle those dirty seasonal tasks that will make your house shine. Wash the windows, clean out the gutters and power wash the porch.

10. Replace the heavy woolen throw on your couch with something lighter for the season. Linen throws are a great choice as they offer just a touch of warmth on chilly spring mornings.

11. Switch up the hand soap in the bathroom to something with a clean, fresh scent. Citrus scents such as lemon and wild orange are yummy choices.

12. Get your hands dirty and dig around in your garden beds or flower pots. Enjoy the sensation of the warm earth between your fingers.

13. Plant something! It can be as simple as starting a few seedlings.

14. Clear out the coat closet of the winter woolens. Tidy up the space and welcome in your spring coats!

15. Tuck a twenty dollar bill into your winter coat before you pack it away for the season. Forget about it, so you can delight in its discovery later on.

16. Wash your window coverings and open the windows to let in the fresh spring air.

17. Pussy willows might not be colorful, but they make sweet spring arrangements.

18. Polish your winter boots before you store them away.

19. Dry clean your winter coats. Hang them nicely in a spare closet so they are wrinkle free and in perfect condition when the cold weather arrives.

20. Don't bother storing winter attire that you know won't fit next year. Your kids are growing! If you are certain they will soon outgrow the snowsuit and boots, clear them out of your house before they become clutter.

21. Take advantage of the warmer temperatures and explore a new part of town. Enjoy your own company and the delicious feeling of anonymity.

22. Clean out the fridge and fill it with the first spring greens from your local farmers' market.

23. Freshen up the coffee table with new picture books from your personal stash or the library. Gardening books and spring-inspired décor magazines will get you in the spirit of the season.

24. Take advantage of the spring cleanup in your community. Municipalities often offer curbside pick-up of larger items this time of year.

25. Spring is the perfect time to make baby plants. Take advantage of the growing season by propagating your house plants. Expand your own collection by sharing and exchanging clippings with friends.

# Summer

1.  Create an easy, breezy summer vibe by keeping your counters, tables and surfaces free and clear of clutter.
2.  Create a decorative display with seashells and welcome the beach right into your home.
3.  Wildflowers are in season! Scavenge the roadside and have fun bringing home unique bouquets that can't be bought in a store.
4.  Download a wildflower identification app on your phone so you can learn the names of your favorites!
5.  Take advantage of the sun's clean energy and dry your laundry on the line. Delight in this opportunity to bring the sweet smell of fresh air into your home.
6.  Create a small outdoor nook to take advantage of the nice weather. Drink your morning coffee outside.
7.  Put up a hummingbird feeder. Summer is the perfect season to admire these beauties from the comfort of your porch.
8.  A ripe and vibrant bowl of garden tomatoes makes a perfect summer centerpiece.
9.  Spend a lazy summer afternoon scouring your lawn for four leaf clovers. You'd be surprised how easy they are to spot when you are looking. Tuck your treasure into one of your favorite books, to be discovered unexpectedly in the future.

10. Take a summer vacation from the news and social media. Shut off your WIFI for a day and force yourself to unplug.

11. Bring the scents of the season into your home. Make a point of using summer-inspired candles and essential oils to elevate the atmosphere indoors. Beach roses, lavender and peony are some of my favorites.

12. Take the opportunity to gather summer blooms at their peak. Have fun experimenting with potpourri recipes. You will savour these sweet reminders of summer in the cold months ahead.

13. Take advantage of the nice weather and dine al fresco whenever possible. It doesn't have to be fancy. An easy picnic on the lawn can feel luxurious and elegant in its simplicity.

14. When the weather is hot, many people crave lighter meals. Use the opportunity to take a break from your kitchen duties and opt for easy summer salads that can be thrown together on a whim.

15. It can be difficult to motivate yourself to be productive and efficient during the summer. Add any extra touches to your home office space that will make you look forward to sitting at your desk. You can never go wrong with a generous bouquet of fresh flowers.

16. You don't have to have a giant vegetable garden in your backyard to enjoy a taste of summer at home (unless you want to!) Plant a few pots of fresh herbs

and cherry tomatoes. They are easy to maintain, pretty to look at, and add fresh seasonal flavour to your homecooked meals.

17. Switch out your heavy quilts and blankets. Dress your bed in a light summer coverlet so you feel more comfortable and sleep more soundly on hot summer nights.

18. Take advantage of the dry, hot weather to tackle certain household chores. Paint the deck or freshen up the trim. Schedule services such as chimney sweeping and furnace maintenance, so you are well-prepared when the cooler months arrive.

19. Dress at home as you would on a dreamy, Mediterranean holiday. Flowy dresses and chic tunics are cool and easy to move around in, but add an elevated vibe to your time spent at home.

20. Fill your living space with the sounds of summer. Create a summer playlist of music that will immerse you in the mindset of the season. This could be anything from Vivaldi's *Summer Concerto* to The Beachboys!

21. Deal with annoying pests around your home. Pick up a set of ant traps during your next trip to the hardware store before they take over the kitchen.

22. Make evenings on the patio more enjoyable with a set of citronella candles to ward off mosquitoes and other nippy creatures of the night.

23. Stock your freezer full of summer goodness so you can enjoy a taste of the season throughout the year.

Strawberries, blueberries and raspberries all freeze well, and make delicious additions to smoothies, porridge and muffins.

24. Run through the lawn sprinkler when you need to cool off.

25. Keep the freezer stocked with a plentiful supply of ice cubes. There is nothing more refreshing than ice cold water on a hot day.

# Autumn

1. Invite the brilliant colors of the season into your home by decorating your mantle or table top with vibrant gourds of all shapes and sizes.

2. It's the perfect time of year to burn your spicy scented candles with flavours of cinnamon, pumpkin, apple and cloves.

3. Many of us head into back-to-work mode when fall arrives. It's a great time to tackle that list of annoying little home issues when you are feeling productive.

4. Pick yourself up some new stationery supplies during the back to school sales. Set your home office up for productivity and efficiency.

5. Seek out ways to make fall yard work fun. Rake a large pile of leaves, and just for old times' sake, jump in and enjoy.

6. A bowl of bright red apples makes a simple, enticing and healthy centerpiece.

7. Pile firewood with a sense of gratitude for the warmth and comfort it will provide.

8. Autumn is a busy time with new schedules to adjust to. Make the dinner hour a bit easier by treating yourself to the odd package of meal kits. For added enjoyment, delegate the meal prep to another member of the household.

9. Gather a collection of colorful fallen leaves to take home. Carefully press them with a warm iron and wax paper to preserve their beauty.

10. Tuck a few fiery red leaves between the pages of one of your favorite books. Enjoy their beauty next time you crack open the cover.

11. Stock your freezer with meals that can be easily defrosted. They will be much appreciated during this busy time of year.

12. Find a spot to plant a few fall bulbs. You will be thankful for your efforts come spring.

13. Switch up your breakfast menu to include something warm and comforting. A soothing bowl of porridge is a great way to kick off your day with an energizing boost of nourishment.

14. Enjoy cleaning up the yard and garden beds in the absences of biting bugs. The cool air is refreshing!

15. Clean out your bathroom vanity and toss anything old or expired. Switch to beauty products that are more appropriate for the falling temperatures. Choose heavier creams and cleansers that will add more moisture to your complexion.

16. It's the perfect time to reorganize your closet. Have fun pulling out all your cool weather clothes from storage. Jeans, sweaters and boots are back in season!

17. Wash all your summer clothes before tucking them in storage. You don't want sweat stains setting into the fabric.

18. Dress up your doorstep with a few bright orange pumpkins.
19. If you live in the northern hemisphere, autumn is the perfect time to declutter your home from top to bottom. It will feel wonderful heading into the holiday season with a clean slate.
20. Go for a walk in the woods to collect pinecones, acorns and chestnuts. Display them in a beautiful bowl on the coffee table.
21. Enjoy the opportunity to get outside while the weather is still comfortable. It's always nice to take a break from your home environment.
22. Gather together all your favorite mugs and teacups. Enjoy your morning tea or coffee even more by choosing one that suits your mood for the day.
23. Switch up the color palette around you. Choose earthy shades and jewel tones for your clothing, makeup and table linens.
24. Meal plan with seasonal produce in mind. Your family's dining experience at home will be elevated by the bounty of the fresh fall harvest.
25. Add a few drops of a fall-inspired essential oil blend to your cleaning bucket. (Cinnamon, clove and orange make a nice combination.) It will fill your home with a delicious autumn scent.

# A NOTE FROM THE AUTHOR

Thank you so much for reading my book! As a self-published author, I am extremely grateful to each and every one of my readers.

I hope *Elevate Your Life at Home* provided you with some nuggets of inspiration that you can implement into your own homelife. Please keep in mind that our homes don't have to look perfect to serve as safe, loving and cozy sanctuaries. The key to creating an inviting atmosphere at home is to focus on *your own* likes, passions, needs and lifestyle! Adding personal touches with purpose and intention will help create an environment that nourishes your soul. Designing systems that suit your lifestyle and help the day-to-day run more smoothly will bring a sense of ease to your life. Life at home is all about adopting a personalized approach that embraces both who you are, and who you strive to become.

As always, I'd like to remind you that I don't have all areas of my life running like a well-oiled machine at one time! The housework slides, clutter creeps in, and I go through bouts of cranky ungratefulness! I purposefully collected my thoughts in these pages to provide all of us with a place to revisit on occasion. Whenever you wish to reignite your interest in homelife, or are seeking inspiration, please feel free to pull this little book from the shelf. It's meant to offer gentle and friendly reminders whenever we might need them!

If you enjoyed my writing, please check out my other books, *Elevate the Everyday, Elevate Your Personal Style* and *Elevate Your Health.* They offer a similar flavour and are also designed to share motivational tips to bring more joy, comfort, vitality and peace into your life!

I should also mention that I offer a collection of matching blank journals to accompany all my books. If you are looking for a pretty little place to record your thoughts and ideas, they are available on my Redbubble shop (JenMelville.redbubble.com). Please note, I'm not trying to shamelessly push branded products on you! I originally created them as a gift for my mother, but figured it would be fun to open up their availability publicly. Since I enjoy using them myself, I figured others might as well.

Lastly, I have one small favour to ask! I would greatly appreciate it if you would take the time to leave an honest review of this book on Amazon. Not only does this help others discover my work, but it allows me to connect with my readers and gain insight into our shared interests.

Over the past year, a number of you have reached out to me, and I've genuinely enjoyed hearing your feedback and your thoughts on elevating everyday life!

I will now set you on your way to find that fairy inside you, and flex your superhero muscles. Most of all, I wish you a homelife filled with peace, happiness, enthusiasm and magic!


Much love,

Jennifer

# ABOUT THE AUTHOR

Jennifer Melville is a self-published author. She decided to embark on a writing career because she wanted to tap into a community of like-minded individuals who share in her enthusiasm for living well and seeking ways to elevate daily life. She is a professional accountant by trade, who approaches life with an analytical and observant mind. Jennifer has been exploring the concept of elevating the everyday for over twenty years. She is passionate about family, health, fitness, fashion, nutrition, nature and all the beauty life has to offer.

Jennifer lives by the sea in beautiful Nova Scotia, Canada with her husband, two sons and little poodles Coco and Junior.

You can connect with her by email, on her blog, or on her Instagram page.

jenniferlynnmelville@gmail.com

www.theelevatedeveryday.com

www.instagram.com/the.elevated.everyday